PRAISE FOR
The SuperWoman's Guide to Super Fulfillment

"Dr. Jaime Kulaga's debut work is an upbeat, practical, and guilt-free guide to balance and fulfillment. It's expertly crafted to help busy women stay on target with less stress. As Dr. Kulaga shows, balance isn't about learning how to juggle more; it's about focusing on what's important. She teaches powerful techniques to do just that and much more. Take a deep breath, relax, and let *The SuperWoman's Guide to Super Fulfillment* show you how to stand tall and create what *you* really want for your life."

— PATRICIA SPADARO, author of *Honor Yourself:
The Inner Art of Giving and Receiving*

"Kulaga weaves the threads of many concepts into a warm blanket of inspiration, encouragement, and real-world advice for women who aren't on their own priorities list. *The SuperWoman's Guide to Super Fulfillment* blends relatable wake-up call examples with hopeful and achievable snapshots of what a balanced life looks and feels like. Packed with meaningful and practical information, tips, and exercises, it shows how to break free of barrier-building 'shoulds' and 'have tos' in order to live a guilt-free, fulfilling life. A must-read for working women—which is every woman. Highly recommended!"

— PAULA RENAY
The No-Nonse

"*The SuperWoman's Guide to Super Fulfillment: Step-by-Step Strategies to Create Work-Life Balance* gives an insightful look into the busy lives we all lead and offers many tips and solutions that are practical and can be used by anyone, not just women. Dr. Kulaga is a frequent guest on our news programs and has a unique understanding of how to do it all without having to do it all by yourself. This book will help everyone who is seeking work-life balance and time-management skills. Not only will you become more productive, but you and those around you will be happier and more fulfilled by using the skills and techniques in this book."

—JOEY WEST, Bay News 9, Tampa

SuperWoman's
GUIDE
to Super Fulfillment

The SUPERWOMAN'S GUIDE
to Super Fulfillment

....

Step-by-Step Strategies
to Create Work-Life Balance

....

JAIME KULAGA, PH.D.

PIER 99 PUBLISHING

For information, address:

Pier 99 Publishing
8710 W. Hillsborough Ave., Suite 133
Tampa, FL 33615

E-mail: info@Pier99Publishing.com

For foreign and translation rights, contact Nigel J. Yorwerth
E-mail: nigel@PublishingCoaches.com

Library of Congress Control Number: 2014952626

ISBN: 978-0-692-28342-4

10 9 8 7 6 5 4 3 2 1

Cover design: Nita Ybarra
Interior design: Alan Barnett

To women who are trying to balance everything on their plates to keep those around them happy and content.

To women who have found the courage to walk away in tough situations and those who have the courage to stay in tough situations.

To women who put smiles on their faces, nod their heads "yes" even though their minds say "no," and then go into the bathroom to cry.

I dedicate this to you.

CONTENTS

~

INTRODUCTION

WORK-LIFE BALANCE
IS POSSIBLE

$\sim$

Work is more than your 9-to-5 job or your career that pays the bills. Housework is work, relationships are work, taking care of your children is work, even staying in shape is work. For most of us, there's barely enough time to be worker, lover, mom, bill payer, grocery shopper, exerciser, scheduler, chauffeur, cook, caregiver, and teacher and still have a little time left over for balance.

As a result of everything that's on our plate, we often feel there's no way we can actually have a life apart from all those roles. That's when we begin to rationalize that fulfilling all our tasks seven days a week *is* life, not work. When that happens, we become just one more person turning round and round on the perpetual Ferris wheel of nonfulfillment. At first as we begin to take on all our new roles in life, riding the Ferris wheel seems exciting and fun. But over time, we may find ourselves stuck in a repetitive, revolving cycle of busyness with no way to get off the wheel. We literally spend our lives circling around the same things every day, forgetting that our "work" is not our "life."

It doesn't have to be that way. You can create your unique path toward work-life balance. No matter what you've been through before, you can learn to achieve balance, be fulfilled, and take control of your goals and your future. You can become what I call a SuperWoman.

I began touring southern Florida with my SuperWomen workshops in mid-2013. I had been working as a licensed mental health counselor and life coach with a full schedule of clientele who were primarily women. Several of them asked me to help them locate women's groups or workshops. I searched for workshops but couldn't find one that would give my clients an experience they would not forget and that was suited to what they both wanted and needed. I did find some 45-minute workshops that touched on the basics of work-life balance and fulfillment, but my clients already knew the basics. They needed something more advanced. I also found in-depth workshops far away in California or Texas that lasted a week and cost thousands of dollars, but that wasn't practical. In addition to the expense, it would have been unrealistic for the women I was working with to go away and leave their jobs and families. I felt like Goldilocks and the three bears—this one was too little, this one was too much.

One day while sitting at my desk, I got a fabulous idea: Why don't I lead a workshop specifically for women? I have the experience, I have completed research on women, and my clients are asking me for this. (It took a $300,000 PhD degree to figure this out!) That's when I began creating my SuperWoman workshops.

These workshops have empowered and helped women to reach their goals, take responsibility for their lives, and use practical tools to better their personal life stories. The women who attended these workshops are now able to make better decisions, steer the course of their own lives, and find greater happiness. They said that the insights they received were so valuable that I decided to write this book to allow women all over the world to take part in the SuperWoman workshop. *A SuperWoman's Guide to Super Fulfillment* includes many of the concepts and content I discuss in my workshops. By reading each of the chapters and doing the exercises, you'll learn step by step how to become a SuperWoman too.

WHAT IS A SUPERWOMAN?

When I first started leading my SuperWoman workshops, I was asked to write for a motherhood blog. The first comment I received was a question about whether a workshop like mine would only put more pressure on women, who are already trying to fulfill so many responsibilities. *Ah,* I thought, *perfect question!* It allowed me to explain a key concept that is at the core of what you'll learn here: a *super woman* (two words) is entirely different from a *SuperWoman* (one word).

My goal here isn't to help you become a better "super woman." Most likely, you're already a fantastic super woman. You've learned how to juggle multiple tasks at a time day in and day out, in sickness and in health. Learning to juggle more is not the answer and it hasn't brought us more happiness. In fact, research suggests that in the past 40 years there has been a drop in happiness among women. In addition, women are twice as likely to have depression when compared to men. While there have been advances in our society over those years, many women are still overstressed, burned out, and unfulfilled.

What I want to show you is that there is another alternative. I want to help you become a SuperWoman—a woman who knows how to achieve balance between life and work and be personally fulfilled. She realizes that there are times when she has to ride the Ferris wheel to fulfill the life roles she has chosen, but not all day every day. She knows when to step off and enjoy the moments in her life. Being a SuperWoman doesn't mean you won't face challenges—we all do. But instead of being overstressed, burned out, and unfulfilled, you'll have more energy and confidence to deal with those challenges effectively.

EXPLORING YOUR
GOALS, DREAMS, AND EMOTIONS

Women are smart. Most of the time we have the answers—for everyone else, that is. When it comes to knowing what we need, sometimes we don't even know where to begin. We've got other things to do—lots of them. We are the gender that skips using the bathroom when we have to go, just to get one more thing done. We continually sacrifice one more day of sanity, thinking "our day is coming."

The problem is, once we reach the point where we start to think about ourselves, we are already in the habit of putting everyone else's needs first. That habit keeps us stuck on the Ferris wheel of nonfulfillment. When our chance comes to step off the ride, we unconsciously or sometimes even consciously decide to give the carnival boy another ticket to ride in circles again.

Here's an example. Have you ever finished a project or task early or waited on something to come through and found yourself with a few hours of a break—and then you panic? God forbid you actually sit there and enjoy the moment. So what do you do? You literally create unnecessary extra work for yourself to keep busy. That is the result of an addiction to work that many women have. It's also an expression of guilt at perhaps its finest. Guilt that we aren't doing enough to care for others or to keep on top of our tasks at work will stop us from doing things for ourselves. Yet aren't the most successful and fulfilled people the ones who say, "Work hard, play hard"? Successful and fulfilled people do take breaks. SuperWomen take breaks too.

In this book, I'll be asking you to think in new ways, often fun ways, about your life so you can see for yourself that life encompasses much more than what pays the bills or what it takes to care for your loved ones. As you move through the chapters, you will discover the definition of "life" as it pertains to you. Work and life mean something different to each of us. What constitutes fulfillment for me might not be true fulfillment for you. What you need to be in balance will be different from what I need.

I am going to provide you with a variety of very practical tips and exercises for creating your own work-life balance and developing the skills of a real SuperWoman. You'll learn how to identify and focus on your top life roles, say no without feeling guilty, and set smart goals for yourself. You'll learn techniques to boost your self-confidence, create a plan to work through personal obstacles, and reframe your past to work for you in the present. In short, you're going to take back control of your world and start enjoying your life.

I provide the women in my SuperWoman workshops with journals. During the course of the workshop, I ask them to take notes on things they like, feelings that arise, or statements that trigger thoughts, ideas, or emotions. I also ask them to make note of questions they have or anything significant that might come to mind during the four-hour event.

I want you to take part in that experience too. Grab a journal or notebook. As you read this book, you are going to explore and question aspects of your life. Certain emotions may arise or you may rediscover long-lost ideas, passions, or concerns you once had. Whatever comes to mind that you feel is important to you, write it down. Throughout this book, I provide examples of concepts and tools you can use in the areas of marriage, dating, children, and employment. If a specific example doesn't seem to pertain to you, that doesn't mean you should dismiss all the processes or techniques provided in that section. Try to take each example and apply it to other areas of your life as you reflect on and journal about these concepts. Lastly, feel free to write your notes right on the pages of this book as thoughts occur to you.

Holding in your thoughts and ideas as you explore your desires and search for fulfillment will not help you. It will just put you right back where you are now—at the starting line. You've had many ideas, goals, and dreams in your life. Your day-to-day agenda, however, has forced you to push those personal goals into a file in the back of your mind because you think "I don't have time for that." That file might be a bit dusty now or maybe you've even lost track of it. Together we are going to recover it. The more you take notes in this book, are interactive during activities, and use your journal, the more fulfillment you will find. I also encourage you to complete the activities or exercises at the end of each chapter before moving on to the next chapter. That will help you begin to put in place empowering new habits and set the foundation for what comes next.

Even after reading this book, I recommend that you keep journaling. Try to write in your journal at least three times per week. Journaling not only helps let out built-up emotions from the day, but it also helps you think through issues before you act and avoid impulsive decision making. Write down the decisions you are contemplating in your journal and go back to that entry in a day or two. Reread what you wrote. Ask yourself: Does that still sound like a good idea?

Journaling will also help you note your patterns of behavior. For example, if you get anxious frequently, I suggest journaling about when you feel anxious and the activities and thoughts leading up to those feelings. It may take days or weeks to observe patterns of behavior. Be patient. Creating new habits that lead to fulfillment is a process. That process is part of your life journey.

Let's get started. Grab your capes, future SuperWomen—you are about to embark on a journey toward fulfillment and balance!

~

You must have control of the authorship of your own destiny. The pen that writes your life story must be held in your own hand.

—Irene Kassorla

CHAPTER I

WHAT ARE
YOUR TOP LIFE ROLES?

∾

How many life roles are you balancing in your life right now? When I lead my SuperWomen workshops, one of the first things I do is ask the women who have joined me to take out a notecard and list all the life roles they play—any role that consumes their time and energy. On average, women tend to list 20 or 30 life roles. Life roles can be anything from mother, wife, or daughter to laundry doer, friend's therapist, or dog walker.

Unfortunately, I have yet to see a woman write "me" on her list of life roles. When I ask the women, "Did you make the list?" they often reply, "Oh, I am supposed to be on here too?" Laundry doer makes the list almost every time though. We feel guilty for not doing the laundry or not satisfying a spouse, but we don't feel guilty for not doing something for ourselves. That is a perfect recipe for lack of fulfillment and, in later life, depression.

Another symptom that the "life" has gone out of our work-life balance is that we do not know what would really fulfill us. In my life-coaching sessions with women clients, I rarely get an answer to the following question: "What do you like to do, just for you?" If the women do answer, here are typical responses: yoga, massage, pedicure, nap. Those activities are wonderful, but come on, ladies, isn't there something else that you would like to do for yourself—something that would provide long-term gratification and satisfaction? A pedicure is not going to provide life fulfillment. It only provides immediate fulfillment. I am a mother, so I fully understand that we might pay someone $100 to let us nap for 15 minutes occasionally. We do get relief from the nap, but then what? We wake up only to jump back on the ever-revolving Ferris wheel more quickly.

LETTING GO OF GUILT

There are probably many things we would like to strive for or engage in, but many of us have been conditioned to push harder for other people instead. We're very busy doing all the things that we believe "have" to get done, like cleaning the house and, of course, doing the laundry. The things that "have to get done" are, in actuality, part of a habit we have created for ourselves through the choices we have made.

Those choices are all too often driven by guilt. Words like *must, should, have to,* and *ought* fill us with guilt and anxiety. Women despise feeling guilty, so to avoid those feelings we satisfy the "shoulds" in our lives before we satisfy ourselves. What makes the problem worse is that when we do take time to focus on ourselves, we usually have a sense of guilt for doing so. That's a double-edged sword: we're damned if we do focus on ourselves (we feel guilty) and we're damned if we don't focus on ourselves (we lack long-term life fulfillment). Furthermore, we don't often see our own needs or desires as a "must." When I tell women that they themselves need to become a "must" in their own life, a lightbulb goes on in their heads. "I guess I never thought of that," they say.

If our personal perspective is that doing the laundry is something we "have" to do and that we don't "have" to focus on ourselves, we "have" a problem. It's not that we should stop doing the tasks that need doing to support and care for our loved ones. The problem comes when those everyday chores *always* take priority. Consistently satisfying the less important "musts" and "shoulds" as a priority threatens our life fulfillment.

You can begin to turn around the habit of ignoring your own needs and desires by avoiding the use of guilt-ridden and anxiety-ridden words like *have to, must, should,* and *ought.* Eliminating those types of words will reduce feelings of guilt, even unconscious feelings of guilt that you aren't aware of. Take a second to think about all the different phrases you say each day in which a *must, should, have,* or *ought* is attached, such as "I really *should* do X and Y," "I really *should have* X or Y," or "Oh, I *have* to X and Y."

You are brainwashing yourself all day when you do that. You are literally planting seeds of guilt and anxiety into your own head hundreds of times per day. Doing anything in life hundreds of times per day is going to create a habit. In this case, you are now in a habit of provoking your own guilt and anxiety.

I want you to really focus on how many times each day you use those words. Work diligently to change the way you talk out loud and in your head. The only thing you *have* to do is breathe air. You *want* to do the laundry. Believe it or not, laundry is a *want*, not a *have*. Change words of guilt into words of desire: "I *want* to do X and Y" or "I *desire* to X and Y." This way, if you don't do the laundry or cook dinner for the night, your level of anxiousness or guilt will be decreased. Perhaps now you will have the energy to focus on something you *have* to do, like work on you. It is okay to skip cooking dinner a couple times a week to work out, walk on the beach, or do something fulfilling. The only time you need to use the word *have* is when you are talking about having to focus on something for yourself or if you are drowning and *have* to have air.

Fear Kills Our Dreams

On our individual journey of finding out what "life" means to us, we first need to learn about what might hold us back from trying to discover what we are truly passionate about or what we want out of life. Fear, especially for women, is a major obstacle.

When I first began writing this book, I was listening to the audio of *Lean In* by Facebook's chief operating officer Sheryl Sandberg. It's a must read for women who want to be empowered and who want to empower other women. Sandberg talks about the importance of women being aware of their status in society and how women can overcome challenges to become more equal to men in the workplace.

At one point early on in her book, Sandberg calls attention to the factor of fear, quoting an important observation by Ellen Bravo, director of Family Values at Work Consortium, that many women "are not thinking about 'having it all,' they're worried about losing it all." "Fear," says Sandberg, "is at the root of so many barriers that women face."

Those statements made me think about how fear affects women in many ways. How different would our lives or perspectives in decision making be if we did not fear losing something—losing likability, a lover, a friend, respect, our job, our children, etc.? What kinds of bold choices would we make if fear wasn't in the equation?

The research I completed during my doctoral program on women and abandonment also pointed to the role of fear in women's lives. Doing that research was an amazing experience for me because I was able to delve into women's thought processes and emotions about abandonment and relationships. The ultimate way to understand our experiences is to have a knowledge of what is known as "the essences." The essence of a person is revealed when we get down to that person's basic nature and learn what really drives them. The essence is the underlying issue, so to speak. For example, let's say you are studying a group of angry men and you want to know the source of their anger. The underlying essence might not be anger at all but anxiety from X,Y, or Z. After in-depth research, you discover the real issue at hand—not anger but anxiety.

The results of my study with a specific group of women showed that the common, underlying essence of the women's experiences in adult intimate relationships was fear. This fear stemmed from repeated abandonment or fear of abandonment throughout their childhood and adult years. Fear has been rightly described as *false evidence appearing real.* Even though what causes the fear is not always real, fear can become a pattern and habit, a way of life. It can also become the underlying essence or barrier to our fulfillment.

What do women fear? Research as well as my personal experiences working with women have shown that many women fear feelings of guilt and loss. From early in life, women internalize losses. Studies show that when fathers are absent from the home due to divorce or abandonment, girls are more likely to see that loss as due to something that is wrong with them. That may be the beginning of the fear of loss that some women have. Of course, women also take a huge hit to their self-esteem with that type of internalization.

General Patton once said, "Fear kills more people than death." The reality is, death kills us once, but fear kills us over and over again. That could pertain to a lot of different things, but for the purposes of this book think about it in terms of your life balance and fulfillment as a woman. If you fear the feeling of guilt that comes when you do something for yourself or fear losing something or someone if you venture out to explore life, you are not living life. Every time you fear guilt or loss, you are killing a dream you have for your life. Eventually, that particular pattern of thought (we desire something for our life, let fear destroy the idea, then cease moving forward) becomes a pattern of self-destruction and self-sabotage. Fear is a significant issue that you'll learn more about dealing with throughout this book. For now, try to recognize when and in what circumstances fear is a factor that holds you back.

THE HABIT OF PUTTING OTHERS FIRST

As women begin creating families of their own, they often have less time to do the things that once provided them with a sense of fulfillment. That makes sense to an extent. When we add a life role or commitment to our lives, we must drop an existing life role or commitment. But to lose oneself almost completely in that process can create anger, depression, and a lack of fulfillment.

Initially, most women enjoy giving themselves to their new lives. We enjoy making the husband happy and playing wife. Then we have a baby and find ourselves overjoyed with all the new blessings. During this exciting time, you might consciously give up things you like. You don't mind because this is your family and, honestly, playing house is kind of fun. As time passes, you may find yourself giving up more things that you like and making sacrifices that you sometimes don't want to make. And, of course, society is wonderful at making women feel guilty for choosing themselves over their families. How dare we!

It is at this very point, when sacrifice becomes a habit, that you have bought your first block of tickets for the Ferris wheel ride. Life becomes consistent, structured, and cyclical. As you continue to pass up moments where you could be doing something for yourself, you minimize the opportunities that could lead you to identify what you want and what would fulfill you. Before you know it, when asked what you like or what would provide you with fulfillment, you respond with "I don't really know" or "yoga, massage, pedicure, nap."

Should we just not tend to our families? Should we put aside what "has" to get done in order to be selfish? Yes and no. There is work and there is life. You must find your balance. Spouses, children, and work are very important, but so are you.

By our very nature, we are caring, nurturing, and communal. In no way should we give up those characteristics, but here is the issue: *kindness ≠ doormat.* By nature, people are takers. You cannot fault people who take from you. If you are going to give and give and give, people are going to take and take and take.

Set boundaries. Here is where the phrase "Fool me once, shame on you. Fool me twice, shame on me" comes into play. As you get into a habit of giving and putting others first, you begin to minimize yourself and forget what would even fulfill you. You watch yourself giving without even knowing why you are giving or how you got into this place. It is the habit, the structure, and the cyclic nature of your life that causes you to give again, almost unknowingly. Someone, please halt the Ferris wheel! Sometimes, we find ourselves in the middle of a panic attack just because we forgot X or Y on "our" to-do list when the X or Y is really taking on extra work for someone else. We are actually stealing other people's to-do lists and doing them. Stop stealing—it's illegal.

GIVING ATTENTION TO YOUR TOP LIFE ROLES

The average person takes on 15 to 25 life roles. Women reluctantly find themselves on the higher end of those figures.

We like to be liked. When another life role is added onto our plate via child, husband, friend, family member, or boss, we agree verbally but may be screaming *no* on the inside. The problem is, people can't hear our thoughts. They take our word. This goes back to the concept of fear. Because we don't want our child, husband, friend, family member, or boss to reject us, be upset with us, or not call upon us the next time they need our help, we opt to take on the next challenge, then go to the bathroom and cry.

Reality check: women and men alike can typically only handle about five life roles. Take a strong look at all your life roles and evaluate which five are most important to you and your fulfillment in life. Let's say your top five life roles are you, mother, wife, caregiver, and employee. If you focus heavily on those areas, you will not only feel better personally, but the people involved in those areas of your life will give you heightened respect and understanding when you seek your own personal fulfillment. You will need that support in your journey toward super fulfillment.

The first activity at the end of this chapter will help you evaluate your top life roles and starting setting priorities. As you learn to say no to tasks outside your key life roles, you are setting boundaries with those you love and with those you can't stand. The people who are part of your strong and valuable support systems will actually be okay with you saying no to taking on certain tasks. Good supports will tell you to say no. If saying no is hard for you, practice saying no to those you feel safe with. Write in your journal some premade responses to those who consistently ask you to take on additional roles you do not want to take on.

Sometimes, as women, we have a very hard time saying no to men. Perhaps it goes back to the fear of loss. You might think that if you stand up to your male boss, you could lose your job. That is a real fear. Women are awesome at compromising though. Use your very nature to your advantage. Try compromising with a boss when you are asked to take on an extra role. Women are also communal. If you enjoy doing things as a team, try getting the family involved in a project you are taking on. On the job, encourage co-workers to take part in what you are doing. Do not feel bad when you need to delegate a task.

You'll also find that once you can give the necessary time and attention to those in the key areas of your life, you will be better able to handle the less-fulfilling or less-demanding roles, like laundry doer and PTA mom. Why is that true? As you begin to focus more on your top life roles, decreased feelings of guilt will free up more energy for you to focus on other tasks in your life. Also, as you spend quality time with the people and things you care about most, you will notice that you don't have to give so much time to each person or task.

Quality time is dedicated time. If you spend hours on the computer or phone while in the same room with those you love, that would be quantity but not quality. In that example, you are spending a lot of time with those you love, but not dedicating your attention to them or focusing on them. Attention and focus is what the people who are part of your top life roles need. So free up some of your time by providing those you care about with quality time.

If nighttimes are for your children, make 6 p.m. to 9 p.m. about your children and not about work. Avoid answering phone calls, watching television, or doing anything that the children would perceive as you not spending time with them. Instead of spending four hours of computer time while you are sitting in a room with your children multitasking, give them less time but give them your undivided attention. Take interest in what they are doing in life. Bond with them. The same thing goes for the other key people in your life. When you have set aside time for them, give them your exclusive attention. Then your loved ones will be satisfied, you will be guilt free, and you will notice that you now have more time for tasks that could benefit you.

Something else to keep in mind is that the people who are involved in your key roles must perceive that you are satisfying their needs. While completing research for my dissertation, I read Meg Meeker's book *Strong Fathers, Strong Daughters: 10 Secrets Every Father Should Know.* In one chapter, she discusses bonding between a father and son versus bonding between a father and daughter. Meeker indicated that if a father spent three hours on the couch watching a football game with his son and didn't say one word, he might have bonded with his son. If, however, a father were to spend the same amount of time sitting on the couch with his daughter and not say a word, she might sit there wondering the entire time if he was upset with her because he didn't talk to her. Spending time with your children your way does not necessarily mean that it is satisfying to them. Make sure all the moments you spend with the people in your top five life roles are spent both efficiently and effectively.

It's a simple formula: Who do you most fear losing in your life? Those are the people you want to give your most dedicated time to. What do they perceive as valuable time with you? That's what you need to provide them with.

DELEGATING IS NOT A BAD WORD

As I coach women, I sometimes feel that when I use the word *delegate,* I have cussed them out during the session. Some of the women look at me as if the word must be foreign, while others think I have a devious plan to take control away from them. Women who have a tough time delegating have gotten into a habit of taking on everything themselves.

We create the foundation of this habit at a young age. As young adult women, we began to take on life roles left and right as if we were superheroes. People commended us on our strength and abilities, and it was nice to be complimented and supported by women who were older than we were. Some people told us to slow down, but we couldn't slow down. We had something to prove. We had life planned out and what was ahead of us was exciting and fulfilling. We felt that we could do it all. We skipped the journey and went right for the finish line.

After a while, however, there were days when we were exhausted and wanted a break. As it turned out, the finish line was not the finish line. The finish line was actually the beginning of another quest. Were we being tricked? We began to question ourselves and what happiness and fulfillment really looked like. What we once did that others considered kind now appeared to us as something we were expected to do. You might have even come to expect that you should take on roles that were set in front of you regardless of whether you liked them or not. The truth is that not only can you decline additional life roles, but you can actually delegate some of the responsibilities associated with your current life roles.

From my experiences working with older women, I have found that the concept of delegating is sometimes nonexistent. Sixty years ago, times were different than they are now. Many women were married by 21 years of age and their profession was motherhood. Today, to maintain a household many families need two incomes. Women have adapted to the changing times and many have careers outside the home, but some of us have never let go of the responsibilities of our job *within* the home. We added a major new role but didn't drop a role.

The issue here is that women have taken on a second full-time job—job 1 in the home, job 2 outside the home. Working 80 hours or more per week plus all the stress that comes from having two jobs leads to a decrease in life fulfillment and an increased chance of depression. In extreme cases, depression and leading an unfulfilled life play a role in women's suicide attempts. Here's a startling fact: research shows that women are three times more likely than men to attempt suicide. Women tend to use "beautifying" ways to attempt suicide, such as taking pills. Men tend to use more destructive ways to kill themselves, such as using a gun. Chances of death are higher when a more lethal method is used, which is the reason more men than women die when they attempt suicide. What's important to note, however, is that more women than men *attempt* suicide. Sadly, the group of women aged 60 to 64 has seen the largest jump in suicide rates—a rise of almost 60 percent since 1999.

ARE YOU MISSING THE MOMENT?

One of my aunts is in her 60s. She came from a strong Italian background. She shares stories of helping my nana cook in the kitchen when my aunt was a young girl. One of the responsibilities of cooking was serving the man first.

When dinner was cooked, my aunt and nana would serve my grandfather first, then the two brothers. Once the men were served, my aunt and nana would serve themselves. This pattern has continued throughout the years. When I was younger and would go to my nana's house, my grandfather and father would always be served first.

Today when I am cooking, I serve my children first to get them to calm down and then pass out the rest of the food, sit, and eat. Running two businesses together, my husband and I are forced to be a team. We cook the food together and get it on the table together. We high five at the end of the meal for the sheer fact that we got through another chore and the children are still alive!

When I visit my aunt, I notice that a lot of our Italian tradition still remains with her. As proud as I am of my heritage, I see how her habit of always putting others first before herself impacts her life. On one occasion, my aunt's friend came over and she created a beautiful meal for us all. We were all outside in the pool enjoying the moment, but she was inside cooking. She said that she liked to cook and that it wouldn't take her long. Yet I could see that she was missing "the moment" and that her selflessness and habit of putting others first had literally caused her to miss moments in life that could have led to her feeling more fulfilled.

Women in their 60s have been shaped by stories of strength and resilience. Many women in this group have faced divorces, loss of a spouse, or health issues. These life-changing events often bring attention to our need for life fulfillment. At age 60, just starting to find fulfillment out of life can be scary. Searching for yourself at any point in life is scary, but as we age we have other factors that can interrupt the self-searching process, such as health concerns.

Whether you are an adolescent, are a young adult, or are in later adulthood, pausing to reflect on the moment is essential. Regardless of age or tradition, it is important to enjoy the moments with those you love and care about most. Focusing your time and energy on the little "musts" and "shoulds," such as constantly staying busy in the kitchen cooking, takes away from the "wants" and what could lead you toward feeling fulfilled and enjoying the moment. If you find yourself constantly missing the moments with those you love, I urge you to reconsider how you are spending your time. If you invite people over to spend time with them, enjoy that time with them.

I notice a similar tendency for women to miss the moment as I interact with family, friends, and clients during the holiday season. The women spend so much time prepping, stressing, cooking, serving, and cleaning up that not only do they miss the moment of the holiday season, but they are glad when it's over. During the next holiday season, set boundaries and limit yourself to what you can handle emotionally. Be sure that you enjoy the holiday too. Remember who you are committed to caring for in your top five life roles and don't go overboard serving all the people who are outside the sphere of those roles. Typically, as we stress about serving others outside our top five life roles, we complain to the ones we actually care about most. You do not want your graciousness in pleasing others to become something that burdens those who are truly important to you.

To help you stay focused on the moment and on your priorities, it's a good idea to pause a few times a day to reflect on the situation you are in and what you are experiencing. Check in with yourself to see if what you are doing is aligned with your priorities. Ask yourself: What about this moment do I enjoy? If I am not enjoying this moment, why not? Are my priorities where they should be? Could I delegate some of what I am doing to someone else?

Making Choices Based on Priorities

As new opportunities arise in your life, consider what's happening in your top life roles before choosing to say yes or no to those opportunities. Here is a perfect example of what can happen in our daily lives when we take on extra roles we can't handle and pile too much on our plate. As I was promoting a new business venture, I decided to join a networking group. This was a weekly commitment and required me to meet one-on-one with several people each week in addition to the weekly meeting. I knew up front that there were commitments to being in this group. I kept telling myself that successful people work hard and this was part of what I "had" to do. About one month into the group I was asked to take on a leadership role. There was no pay for this role and I was being asked to give even more of a commitment and more of my time, both of which I did not have.

I was grateful for that opportunity and didn't want to disappoint the group. I also feared (again, notice the concept of fear) that saying no to this opportunity would make it look as if I was not the "super woman" everyone thought I was. As I explained in the introduction, by "super woman" I mean someone who manages to take on and juggle every opportunity that comes her way—*"Here is Jaime, the one who keeps adding to her plate and yet still shines and doesn't fail."* Now I know that the goal is not to be a "super woman," which eventually leads to exhaustion, guilt, unhappiness, and regrets, but a "SuperWoman," who chooses responsibly based on her priority life roles.

Although I may have seemed to others like a master juggler, little did they know that things were failing and I was tired. Worse, I was not satisfying the people who were part of my top five life roles and I felt a lot of guilt about that. So when the gentleman in this group asked me to take on the leadership role, my brain screamed, "Hell *no!* Are you kidding?!" while I heard my voice say, "Yes, I would love this opportunity."

I immediately called my husband and told him what I had done. Not only did he think I was insane and told me to take back my yes, but looking back, I must have caused him disappointment. Being his wife is my top life role. At that point in my life, I wasn't fulfilling my commitments by giving dedicated time to him. Now, with this added commitment, the little time I did have I was choosing to give to a networking group. That was not a responsible choice. I did more harm than good to everyone, even myself, by trying to avoid the guilt of saying no and the fear associated with possibly not being offered a leadership role in the future.

Women work really hard to be credible and gain authority. The one thing you do not want to do as a woman is say yes to something and then take back your word. But that is exactly what I did after joining this networking group. Despite my husband's good advice, I didn't back out right away. Then one month into my leadership role, I began slipping on my commitments. I was not carrying my fair weight in group exercises and I was embarrassed. Not long after I joined the group, I emailed an apology letter to my teammates and resigned from my position and my participation in the group. Not only had I said yes to being part of the group and then turned around and said no, but I had emailed them that I needed to drop out. How impersonal! Afterwards, I felt as if I had lost credibility, and I probably had. I did not mean to fail them. I appreciated everything they had done for me and I liked these people as professionals and some even as friends. It was because of my personal inability to know and understand my boundaries that I did not meet their expectations or my own.

Since that event, I have learned the importance of speaking up. If I had simply acknowledged the leadership offer, been grateful, and politely declined, the people in this group would most likely have respected me more. I've also learned that more opportunities always come up, even if we say no to something that is not right for us at the moment. Before making a decision to accept another role or task, take a step back to reflect on what would be most beneficial for you and the people involved in your priority life roles. When you do that, you'll find that your credibility will go up and your potential for more opportunities will increase.

I later realized that while this networking group was wonderful, based upon who I am and the life roles that were important to me at that time in my life, taking on this new commitment was not something I should have even considered. I was unable to drop a role to add this one and I learned a huge lesson from it.

A few months after leaving the networking group, I was asked to present at an international learning seminar. I knew that the preparation for this presentation was going to take my time and energy in order for it to be a success. I would have to do a lot of prep work, both physically and mentally. I had learned from my networking experience. I wanted to do everything, but I finally admitted and accepted that I couldn't.

So I evaluated my top five life roles and my responsibilities prior to agreeing to present at the learning seminar. I examined which life roles I couldn't change or did not want to change and which I could. Then I made the decision that I would stop offering the SuperWomen workshops for a couple months so I could channel my energy into the new presentation. When that presentation was completed, I added the SuperWoman workshops back onto my plate. I had learned that in order to be effective, I had to drop a role before adding a new one. Women can do anything they want, but they can't do everything.

~

Your most valuable resources are your time, energy,
and attention. What you choose to do or not
to do with them will determine whether
you will thrive or barely survive.

—PATRICIA SPADARO

ACTIVITY

PICKING MY TOP FIVE LIFE ROLES

Take a moment to think about all the life roles you now ful-fill—any role you spend time and energy on. Then write them down on a piece of paper. From that list, choose your top five life roles and write them in the blank spaces below. Note that life role number one has already been added for you.

1. **Me** _____

2. _____

3. _____

4. _____

5. _____

(For a printable version of all the worksheets in this book, go to www.mindfulrehab.com and click on the link that says "SuperWoman Worksheets.")

....

Now that you've taken time to reflect on what your top life roles are, reflect on these questions and write down your an-swers:

- Who or what have you been giving too much of your valuable time to that might not have deserved it?

- Who or what were you giving priority to that is not on your list of top life roles?

- How will dedicating more quality time to the people in your top life roles make you feel happier, more fulfilled, and less guilty?

....

Keeping in mind the five top roles in your life, write down the answer to this question:

- What will I have to stop doing, do less of, or delegate in order to dedicate myself to these roles as my top priorities in life?

SuperWoman Skills

I focus on my top life roles.

A SuperWoman has identified her top five life roles
and makes sure she is number one on that list.

A SuperWoman focuses on giving
100 percent to her top five roles.

A SuperWoman understands the differences
between "kindness" and "doormat."

A SuperWoman does not feel guilty saying no to
people who have mistaken her for a doormat.

A SuperWoman sets boundaries with all people,
even spouses, children, and co-workers.

A SuperWoman makes time to enjoy the moments
with those she loves and cares about most.

A SuperWoman understands that she can do
anything she wants, but she can't do everything.

CHAPTER 2

Making Confidence
a Core Strength

∼

Girls grow up being showered in pink and boys in blue. From early childhood, children are pushed in a certain direction unknowingly and sometimes unwelcomingly. Take the psychology of the color blue. Blue represents reliability and responsibility. It reflects inner security and self-confidence and stands for having direction in life. Pink, on the other hand, represents nurturing, love, and compassion. Pink also reduces feelings of aggression. In fact, research suggests that being surrounded by large amounts of the color pink can literally create a physical weakness in people. Girls grow up to want dolls and wedding dresses, a sign of nurturing and compassion. Boys engage in backyard football and gun fights, enhancing skills like being aggressive and competitive.

Whenever I am asked to speak to women on the topic of work-life balance, there is always one portion of the seminar in which I go around and ask several of the women this question:

"What is the best advice you have ever been given?" Go ahead. Take a moment and answer this for yourself.

During the workshops, the women give answers such as "Never give up," "Find your passion," "Treat others as you want to be treated" or "Do what makes you happy." They share endless quotes, and some really great ones at that. During a seminar I once attended that was led by a man, he asked a similar question to the audience. The first man who responded answered in a way that has always stuck with me. He said: "The best advice I was ever given was given to me by my father when I was a young boy. He told me I must be *aggressive* in life, work, and love." That was such a wakeup call for me. As a male, he had been taught early in life to be aggressive in everything he would do. Women are told to "push hard" and "never give up," but we're rarely ever told to be "aggressive."

Think about the word *aggressive* and what it really means—not the word *tough*, not *strong*, but *aggressive*. Aggression is considered to be almost bully-like, especially if a woman is called aggressive. The sad reality is that there is still discrimination against women. Women are called "bitches" for being overly aggressive and might even lose promotions if they seem to be too pushy or not a "team player."

Do we, as women really want to be known as being aggressive in a society that looks down on pushy women and that is unlikely to change overnight? Given the current reality, probably not because it could backfire on us. I wish that wasn't the case, but changing our culture is a work in progress. We can be a part of the progressive change that is needed, but change won't happen tomorrow.

So if the theories regarding the color pink hold true and pink does reduce aggression, are women at a disadvantage from the start when it comes to navigating and competing one on one with men in the business world, for example? The answer is a resounding no. The good news is that we have the tools that can make us triple aggressive in an incognito way if we just become more self-aware and self-confident. Many women lack confidence, however. They tend to have high levels of self-doubt and are the most critical of themselves. As a Superwoman we can learn to replace those tendencies, both in our personal and professional lives, with some practical confidence-building skills.

CREATING A CONFIDENT MINDSET

One area where women can and should be more aggressive is in pursuing their desires and goals. When we focus on that, when we are fulfilled in life and step off the Ferris wheel, we gain strength and confidence. That confidence is, in effect, our own form of aggression. We do not have to be aggressive in the same way men are, but we can still get results. A woman can make necessary demands, be successful, and get what she wants by showing confidence and standing up for herself using the appropriate language.

When applying for a new job, for instance, a woman can use her confidence the way a man might show aggression in his interview. Let's say that you have a job interview for a promotional position within a company. Go into the interview knowing that you are going to get the job. You are not going to jinx the job if you go in confident! You are actually jinxing the job if you go in *not* being confident. If you behave and talk in an interview with confidence, you instantly give off a vibe that you are strong, powerful, and the right type of aggressive for this new position.

Some women pregame their interview with a lack of confidence by saying to themselves and others, "I hope I get this job" or "I really need this job." Instead, affirm "I have worked my ass off for this position—it is mine!" If you act and speak as if you are needy, you're not going to get the advancement. If you are confident, you will. Don't compare yourself to the guy who is the boss's favorite or the woman who has more experience than you. Maybe one of them will get the position in the end, but if you go in with that mindset from the start, your brain will try to prove itself right.

I always tell my clients, do not live the same pain twice. If you create anxiety and tell yourself, "I won't get the job," and then you in fact don't get the job, then you have lived the pain twice—once before the outcome is settled and once after you found out you didn't get the job. And if you tell yourself, "I won't get the job," and then you *do* get the job, you've lived the pain initially for no reason. In both cases, the stress isn't helping you at all. This goes for everything in life. Do not stress out until it's time to stress out.

Take a moment to think about the different times in your life when you worried unnecessarily or worried before an event even took place. Now think about the times in your life that the event you were worried about went smoothly and nothing negative happened. How many times did everything go fine or turn out even better than fine in the end? How much unnecessary energy did you spend worrying? In place of that worrying, what else could you have done for yourself or done to contribute to your fulfillment?

HIGHLIGHT YOUR SUCCESSES

As women, we are really good at seeing the good in others and the bad in ourselves. If we mess up or end up not being right about something, we are critical of ourselves. Because of this habit, our confidence is depleted much more quickly when we make a so-called mistake than it is boosted when we do something that increases our confidence.

During the low points of your life, even if you caused them, reflect on the good decisions you have made in the past and in recent months. To prepare for that, create a list of your successes when you are strong and on a good path (you can use the worksheets at the end of the chapter to make your list). When you become vulnerable or tired, take out your list and reflect on your good choices.

Why is it a good idea to make a list of lifetime successes and recent positive decisions or choices? Our mind sometimes plays games with us. When self-doubt rears its ugly head or our confidence drops, we can downplay our successes over time. If one of your major life successes was "Graduating College," but this event was ten years ago, you may find yourself rationalizing that you haven't had any major successes in a decade. This is by far untrue, but when the mind is in an intense emotional state, it is hard to see ourselves and our lives clearly. Staying aware of your pattern of good choices by taking the time to write down and reflect on them helps boost your confidence levels. This way, you come across as more confident when you have to make bigger decisions or interact with authority figures.

Many of the big decisions in a woman's life involve interaction with men, and confidence can be your greatest ally when you are up against an aggressive male. I have found that when women are most vulnerable in life, they are often placed in front of a man. For example, in situations of divorce, loss of a job, or death of a loved one, we might find ourselves seeking out an attorney, accountant, or someone in law enforcement. Those are male-dominated fields. When a woman has to make a major life-changing decision, there is a high likelihood that at some point she will be guided, at least in part, by a man. Working on your confidence levels on a daily basis will help you get ready for those kinds of encounters.

GOOD DECISION MAKING IS NOT IMPULSIVE

When we present ourselves to others as vulnerable or emotional, people will sweep in and guide us in the direction they think is best without really knowing what we need or want. Everyone has a motive. People might not want to hurt you deliberately, but the fact is, you are the only one who lives your life and walks in your shoes. No one really knows what is best for you except you. If someone makes a decision on your behalf and it's the wrong choice, they march on and you are stuck figuring out the rest.

When you are in a vulnerable state, bring your confidence to the table. If you feel that you are being pressured or your gut is telling you that something is not right, you can say no, get a second opinion, or tell the person giving advice that you need to reflect on the situation and will come back to it.

I always tell my clients, *no impulsive decisions!* This goes for breaking up with boyfriends, leaving a job, firing an employee, investing in stock, anything. When women make impulsive decisions, it is typically out of emotion. It's like being at the supermarket, where you see those little end caps at the checkout with the mascara, magazines, gum, and soda. When you are in line and quickly grab a magazine, it's a last-minute impulsive purchase. It's not really what you wanted when you came to the supermarket, but based on instant gratification and impulsivity, you grabbed the item.

When you go home, it's not the end of the world if you regret buying the magazine—it was four bucks. However, if you impulsively break up with a loved one, that is going to cost you more than the price of a magazine. Breaking up was not really what you wanted, but you did it based on instant gratification, wanting to get in the last word or prove a point.

In coaching sessions, I ask clients who often make impulsive decisions to take part in a painting activity. When people impulsively break up a relationship, they often say hurtful things that they do not mean. During the painting activity, I ask my client to take a paint brush and spread around blots of various colors on a white piece of paper. The individual blots of colors represent a time when the client said or did something to someone that was hurtful. Once she has completed this task, I politely ask her to take a rag and erase all the blots of paint and make the piece of paper white again.

Needless to say, this can't be done. The point of the activity is that when you say or do something to hurt someone, even if you take back your words and apologize, you have scarred that person. Impulsivity scars. It scars your partner, it scars you, and it scars the entire relationship.

Making impulsive decisions also decreases our confidence because those kinds of decisions, with little thought behind them, are not strong decisions. Even worse, if you end a relationship abruptly but really don't want to, as you beg to get back together with your partner, you use time and energy. You also forfeit some of your personal control and have ruined your credibility within the relationship. Clearly, that's not a confidence-boosting process. The more you act impulsively, the more you will find that your decision-making process is not very good. Repeated patterns of poor decision making decrease a woman's confidence.

To increase your confidence, take more time to reflect on situations before making a decision. Reflection takes more than 20 minutes. Reflection can take days, weeks, or even months of journaling and talking to those in your support systems to come to a rational, clear-headed, open-minded decision. Get in the habit of processing decisions in this manner. That way, when you are in a vulnerable state or are confronted by someone who appears to be stronger than you, you will already have established a habit of listening and then taking your own time and space to reflect before coming to a conclusion.

You Don't Have to Be Perfect

Raising children is another area in life where women need to be confident. In therapy, I have worked with mothers who feel responsible for all the wrong their children have done. One mother I worked with had an adolescent daughter who was acting up in school and the mother thought it was all because of her divorce years ago. My client had been abused verbally and physically, and she still says that if she would have "stuck it out" for her daughter, her daughter wouldn't be having "all this trouble" in school.

As much as I value marriage and think that couples should work through problems, abuse should never be tolerated. Just as children only get one life, so do you. It is not selfish to walk away from abuse. Of course, there is much more to walking away than actually walking away. There are real fears and the need for support and protection that come along with this process. Walking away from any relationship that is hurtful takes confidence and courage. That's one reason many women stay in abusive relationships. It is not easy to pick up and begin again.

If you are a woman who has walked away from abuse, you should reward yourself. In the situation with this mother who felt guilty about her daughter, maybe the divorce did play a role in the daughter's acting out. But it is not fair, nor is it reality, to say that the divorce is the only reason for her behavior. Adolescents are well aware of the choices they make. They are also influenced by other extraneous variables such as peers, the educational system, hormones, and simply trying to find their own identity. Since there are so many other variables that could be playing a role in this teenager's behavior, the mother should not place blame solely onto one source, herself.

Even if we could somehow identify that this young girl's acting out was 100 percent because of my client's choices, then I suppose my client would find that she was an imperfect mother. Not perfect? Yes! Ladies, we are not perfect. SuperWomen have imperfections and experience failures too. By thinking that you have to be perfect at anything in life, you create a barrier to your goals and life fulfillment. Nothing and no one is perfect. Don't spend your life trying to be something that doesn't exist. One of my favorite quotes is from Thomas Edison, who said, "I failed my way to success."

How to Prep for Successful Interactions

The way women communicate is also important in demonstrating confidence. Communicate with confidence to get the results you desire, results that will lead to your life fulfillment. Sometimes our forms of communication can discredit or embarrass us. The way that men talk and communicate is not how women should talk and communicate. Women are different, and society sees us as being different.

No, it is not fair that Tom can be confrontational with the boss and somehow still be promoted, whereas in the same situation you will be fired or ridiculed, but life is not fair. Use the incognito aggressive skills that I talked about earlier. To move yourself forward, instead of being confrontational use your strengths of being determined and being communal.

Be confident. If you want something from your boss, take time to scope out what type of personality he has. When was your boss most receptive to you? Why was he receptive? What did your nonverbal communication communicate? If you can prep for a situation that involves an important request or action, you will set yourself up for success.

If you are preparing to ask for something, analyze who you think will be at the meeting, know ahead of time what your objective is, and rehearse how to respond to critical comments so that you are not cornered. Do not walk into situations leading with emotion. Being overly excited, anxious, sad, or downright angry can create a negative situation for you and even deplete some of your hard-earned credibility. In addition, never let someone else put you down in order to raise themselves up. Speak up with confidence to protect yourself. Speaking up with confidence is different than speaking up with emotion. Use that incognito aggression so that you maintain your credibility and so that the accomplishments you have created are noticed.

I have learned that when we as women are communicating with others it's best not to start out with "I think" or "I feel," especially in business. Changing that habit was very challenging for me initially and is still something I need to be cognizant of when I speak. The reason to avoid those phrases is that business is business and we should keep our feelings and emotions out of it.

I recommend applying the rule of not using "I think" or "I feel" in our personal communication too. Here's my theory. Many women discredit themselves, have low self-esteem and self-confidence, and frequently doubt themselves. If a woman who frequently doubts herself says, "I *think* I should write a book," she has placed doubt in the very context of her life goal. If she already doubts herself in general, then in her mind anything she *thinks* she would like to do could be wrong. We are much more likely to succumb to riding the Ferris wheel when we couple our guilt about putting ourselves first with self-doubt. If you really want to write a book, say, "I *will* write a book." You have now backed up your life goal with confidence and determination—two incognito-aggressive womanly characteristics.

As you work on boosting your confidence with the tips in this chapter, remember that it's okay not to be perfect and it's okay to ask for help along the way. Remember that women are different from men. As a SuperWoman, you can be successful and find fulfillment by using your confidence and watching your language so that it reflects your confidence. And if you are finding that your life consists primarily of work, it is time for you to become a bit more aggressive—I mean confident—as you pursue your own personal fulfillment in life.

～

*No one can make you feel inferior
without your consent.*

—ELEANOR ROOSEVELT

MY SUCCESSES AND POSITIVE CHOICES

Reflect on your overall successes in life as well as positive decisions or choices you have made within the past 6 to 12 months. Write down those past successes and recent choices in the worksheets below.

Reminding yourself of your successes and the good choices you have made will help boost your confidence in the present. Turning to this list in the future when you are discouraged or feel self-doubt about a particular issue will also help bolster you.

I want you to visually see all the major successes in your life so you can realize that you have accomplished major feats. I also want you to see more recent decisions and choices you have made that were positive so that you are confident that you are indeed capable of succeeding at new feats in the present.

My Major Life Successes:
(list a minimum of 10)

1. _____

2. _____

3. _____

4. _____

5. _____

6. _____

7. _____

8. _____

9. _____

10. _____

My Recent Good Choices or Decisions:

(list a minimum of 10 and must be within past 6 to 12 months)

1. _____

2. _____

3. _____

4. _____

5. _____

6. _____

7. _____

8. _____

9. _____

10. _____

SUPERWOMAN SKILLS

I call on my confidence as a core strength.

A SuperWoman makes her own decisions.

A SuperWoman speaks out loud and to herself
in ways that build her self-confidence.

A SuperWoman leads with
confidence instead of aggression.

A SuperWoman knows that she
doesn't have to be perfect.

A SuperWoman doesn't make impulsive decisions.

A SuperWoman highlights and stays aware
of her past and recent successes.

CHAPTER 3

The Real Barriers to Fulfillment

~

Before you can move on to explore what you desire in life and how to get it, you first need to know what's been stopping you from pursuing your life goals. Awareness of the self and what's been holding you back from finding fulfillment is essential to growing and finding life balance. When you tell yourself you "can't" do something because of X, Y, or Z, you stop your brain from forward thinking. You cycle around the Ferris wheel yet again. Even if you could find a way to do something for yourself, the word *can't* stops the brain from even trying to find a solution. You think, if it "can't" be done, why even waste time trying?

There are a number of things you might perceive as barriers to moving toward fulfillment, including caring for the important people in your life. I call these "positive barriers." I love my children and husband. To me, they are more important than any goal or life role. Many times, caring for my husband and children *is* my goal. However, that doesn't mean I have to set aside other desires that would help me achieve fulfillment. It's not selfish to say that. It shows confidence in my ability to be a wife and raise my children effectively *and* have my own personal life fulfillment. For instance, writing this book was a life goal for me. I decided I could love my children, take them to school, play with them, and still set aside some alone time for myself to write a book. I had to stay up late to complete the book, but no one said this goal would be easy to accomplish whether or not I had children.

I am a mother, wife, life coach, professor—and now an author. Was I nuts to take on that new task? A little bit, but to keep our sanity and find fulfillment, we have to be nuts sometimes. I didn't have to give up my children in order to pursue my life goals, and you don't have to give up your "positive barriers" in order to find fulfillment. Instead, reframe your thinking so it's a win-win. As you learned in chapter 1, when you commit to setting aside time in your day to fulfill one of your priority life roles, give 100 per cent to it. In the example I just gave, I made sure that the time I spent with my children was dedicated time that they saw as valuable. When I satisfy my children's needs in a way they perceive as satisfying, they are more accepting of me taking time to work on my personal fulfillment.

RELATIONSHIP DYNAMICS

Another barrier to achieving your life goals could be your role as spouse or partner. Your relationship does not have to be a barrier, though, if you give it committed time and attention. What does that mean? If you think that simply being at home is giving your spouse satisfactory time, you are mistaken. I love the saying "The grass isn't greener on the other side. It is greener where you water it."

Just as your children need you to spend quality time with them in order for them to be satisfied, so does your partner. If you have set a date night with your spouse or partner, be present with him. Avoid talking about work or children. Do things during that time alone with one another that you would not normally do in front of the children or at work. Or do things together that you simply don't have time to do otherwise. Intimate moments of physical touch like kissing, holding hands, and making love are of real importance.

Another way to create better relationships so they are not barriers to your personal goals is to understand what your partner needs. In counseling, I suggest that couples read *The Five Love Languages* by Gary Chapman. According to Chapman, we all have a primary love language: Quality Time, Physical Touch, Words of Affirmation, Receiving Gifts, or Acts of Service. If your primary love language is Words of

Affirmation, for example, you may like special things said to you but don't really care too much about receiving gifts. The point is, if each partner is not satisfying the other's primary love language, the marriage can suffer.

Knowing your own personal love language as well as your partner's is not only important for keeping your partner happy, but it is also important to know in times of disagreement. A client of mine whose love language is Words of Affirmation recently got into an argument with her boyfriend while they were in the car. His love language is Physical Touch. The argument was heating up and he could see she was getting ready to open the door and walk away. So he tried to calm her down by touching her arm. She became upset, however, because he was not talking to her and offering her words of love and encouraging her to stay in the vehicle. Instead of reaching out to her in *her* love language, he reached out to her in *his* love language, Physical Touch. What happened? My client got out of the car and walked away. Had they both been aware of each other's preferred form of communication, the end result might have been very different.

There comes a point in every relationship when life and reality set in and your marriage might begin to seem stale. Your marriage is living. If you do not feed it, you risk it dying—dying in the sense of divorce or one spouse feeling unfulfilled and distant. To prevent a situation like this from becoming a problem in your relationship and a barrier to your personal happiness, make it your goal to find the passion again by searching for new areas of adventure within your relationship. Make these new and adventurous activities something you can do within your day-to-day interactions. For example, going zip-lining in Brazil with your spouse is adventurous, but it's not something you can do each and every day. However, creating a love box with "365 reasons why I love you" and pulling out one reason each day can be exciting and fun and something you can do together.

Keep in mind, too, that when you identify your own passion and personal desires and work on your own fulfillment, your marriage benefits. A SuperWoman knows that personal fulfillment also has a positive and uplifting impact on her relationship as a whole.

WHOSE LIFE ARE YOU TRYING TO CONTROL?

In addition to the barriers that come from the positive people in your life, you probably have far more not-so-positive barriers that stop you from reaching your goals and propelling yourself toward fulfillment. There are many such barriers, including striving for perfection, overeating, procrastinating, being overly critical of yourself, pressuring others for consistent reassurance, self-injury, or self-medicating via drugs, prescription pills, or alcohol. I label these as "negative barriers" because they are a form of self-sabotage.

Throughout my years as a therapist, I have found that some of the top barriers that stop women from moving toward fulfillment are the need to control others, anger, and anxiety. In this chapter, we'll zero in on those major barriers. You'll have an opportunity to identify what's been stopping you from pursuing your fulfillment and then to create a plan for how to move through those barriers in the future. Just as the meaning of "life fulfillment" is subjective, so are barriers. Be authentic and honest as you begin to identify your personal barriers. Knowing what your barriers are is half the battle.

One of the key barriers women face is the need to control others. As humans, we have a need and desire to control. It's natural. Control is okay as long as we focus on controlling ourselves and not others. You only get one key to the car that you ride through the journey of life. Hold that key tightly and control your own vehicle. Do not give that key away and let others take control of your journey. Likewise, other people have keys to their own cars. Do not try to take control over other people's cars and change their journey, even if you think that you are right.

The need to control others can be a hard barrier to fess up to. Honestly ask yourself if you are trying to control or change someone. Perhaps you are channeling a lot of your time and energy into getting your boss to see that the way he is operating the office is wrong or into convincing your teenager that his "friends" are really not his friends. That is control. You can provide your boss, teenager, or those you think you need to change with a map to guide their journey, but you cannot drive their car for them.

What would a map look like? You might, for example, go to your boss with solutions that you can implement around the office. Instead of telling your boss that this or that around the office needs to be fixed, try offering him something you can do to add value. If you simply tell your boss what is wrong in the office, you do two things. First, you give him the power to change the problem. Clearly, you do not like the way he is doing things already, so why give him more control to make changes that you probably won't like anyway. Second, by complaining about what's wrong, you are to some degree attacking what he has created in the office. You'll either get brownie points taken away for that or you'll be setting him up to defend why things are running the way they are. The reality is, you don't want to know why things are running a certain way—you want them to change! So figure out what your boss likes and run with that.

Let's say your boss is a numbers guy. He likes when sales go up. Your issue has nothing to do with numbers. What you're concerned about is the gossip in the office and you would like to have more team spirit. Come up with a plan that will help address the gossip as well as his concerns by grabbing your road map and guiding your boss to the best of your ability. Professionally schedule a meeting with him.

During the meeting tell him that you would like to bring up sales numbers in the office and you believe that team building is a great way to do that. Then show him your plan to lead five 30-minute workshops during the next few upcoming team meetings and see what he says. That is putting the control and change in your own hands while giving him a map showing him where you want him to go without actually controlling or using anger to convey your point.

To Create Change, Change Your Reactions

Consider reacting differently to the people you want to change. If you change the direction of your path and they want to follow, they will change paths too. However, your journey and path may not be what is right for them and you must allow them to make their own choices. In reality, the best way to "change" others is not to try and change them at all. Rather, change your response to them and they will consequently be forced to change their response to you. If your typical way of approaching someone has been with demands about what needs to be changed but nothing has ever changed, that's a sign that you need to change your approach.

Here's an example of how a change in approach can create a positive impact on a situation. I once coached an adolescent who wanted a car from her father. I was called in by her father because their relationship was deteriorating, in part because of the constant fighting about her wanting a car. She explained to me that for months she had told her father that she needed a car and given him all the reasons why. Some of the reasons seemed valid. She got good grades, she wasn't into drugs, and she deserved it. The father's stance was that he hadn't owned a car until he was 18, that he had bought his first car with his own hard-earned money, and that his daughter should get a job to pay for a car just as he had.

When working with the young girl, I suggested she approach her father in a different manner if she wanted to get a different response. First, I advised, don't tell him what he needs to do. He is the authority in the family and will continue to defend his rationale since he sees her as the child. She also needed to recognize that the lesson he was trying to teach her was rooted in his childhood emotion and that her approach should not come across as an attack but as empathizing—that is, showing him that she understood how he felt and why.

Additionally, she needed to be aware that when she had listed all the reasons she deserved a car, none of them benefited her father. Quite frankly, from her father's perspective, getting good grades, not doing drugs, etc. was how his daughter should be acting. In other words, she wasn't adding any value to the situation for him by listing reasons like those because he already expected those specific behaviors from her. Essentially, she couldn't use those factors as a bargaining tool when negotiating with him.

This young woman and I discussed a different approach to negotiating. We talked about things that were important to her father and what he currently provided her so she could understand how to use those points when approaching him. I spoke with her about compromise and the idea that sometimes you can get what you want but not exactly the way you want it.

As busy as she was with school, this young lady did not want to take on a part-time job, as her father once had, but she was willing to do some community service. So she proposed to her father a plan to complete community service locally one to two days per week during the school year and 20 hours per week over the summer. By showing her father that she was willing to work above and beyond what he expected from an adolescent, he became more open to the concept of her getting a car.

In this scenario, the young lady changed her response and communication with her father in three important ways. First, she showed she was willing to compromise. She was willing to bend and work for what she wanted as opposed to just stating that she deserved the car. Secondly, she showed maturity. Instead of fighting with him about the car to prove a point, she brought a plan of action to the table.

Lastly, the young lady showed empathy. When she came to the table with her plan of action, she told her father that she understood where he was coming from when he talked about having worked as a young man to buy his first car, and then she explained that community service was a form of work. She also showed gratitude as she thanked him for how hard he was working now, primarily for her. That's empathy. People want to know that you understand them and care about what they are going through. The young lady's new reactions toward her father demonstrated to him that she understood what he was trying to teach her all along. Ultimately, her change in the way she interacted with him changed his reaction to her.

Three months after our coaching relationship began, she got her first car. It wasn't brand new, but it was four wheels and her father paid the majority of the cost. By focusing on what she could change and not pointing fingers at him and telling him what he should do, the young lady received the response she desired.

How can you change your approach to others to create the changes you're looking for? Take a moment now or when you have some quiet time to turn to the first activity at the end of this chapter and reflect on how you might change your actions and reactions to others instead of trying to control them.

Releasing Control and Refocusing

At my Superwoman workshops, I give all the women who attend a generic key. I ask them to design the key or mark it in some way. They can put little beads on it, paint it, or simply put a dot on it with a marker. Then I ask them to put the key on their key ring. Every time they grab their key chain, seeing this key is a quick reminder that *they* hold the key to their life.

I suggest you do the same. Find an old key and make it your new symbol of self-control, decorating it in your own special way. Put it on your key ring as a reminder that you are in control of your life. Only you get to design this key and make it your own. When you try to control someone else, remember that they have designed their own key too. Your design, thoughts, actions, values, and beliefs are your own. You have created your key very differently from the way your spouse, friends, and co-workers have chosen to design their keys. Don't try to tell others how to design the key to their life, which car to drive, and where to park.

Whatever you do, *don't drive someone else's car.* There is way too much responsibility that comes with taking over someone else's life. When you are focused on someone else's life, how can you find time to focus on your own life and fulfillment? Trying to control someone else's vehicle becomes a full-time life role. Trying to control someone else also sets you up for failure. If you try to control someone who doesn't want to change, your attempts will fail. You will find that you have put so much time and effort into working on them that you have forgotten about yourself. That only decreases your personal fulfillment. I have yet to meet one person who can successfully drive two cars at once.

If needing to control other people is one of your barriers to personal fulfillment, take a moment to reflect on why. Why do you feel the need to control others and fear giving up that control? Do you fear not knowing what will happen to you or someone else if you are not in control of the situation or the other person? Do you worry that things will not turn out to be perfect if you don't do them? You learned earlier that it's important to delegate certain tasks that are not in your top life roles. Think about how the need for control might be preventing you from delegating. When you take on all those tasks yourself, the truth is that while you sit around trying to do everything perfectly, the one thing that is not perfect is your level of fulfillment.

If sports-practice chauffeur and your career are in your top five life roles, I do not, of course, recommend delegating those activities all the time. However, you can at times delegate tasks like making dinner, doing laundry, and other lesser roles. If activities like making dinner, doing laundry or yard work, or cooking for school fundraisers are not in your top five life roles, don't add on the extra burden that comes with trying to control the outcome of all those activities. Delegate them and march on to something else that deserves your energy and time.

I've had women tell me that they have to do the grocery shopping because their partners never do it right. Apparently, they believe that you can get a diploma in grocery shopping and that men have not taken the courses to make them eligible to do this task. Guess what, ladies? There is no degree in grocery shopping. This is where we stop sweating the small stuff and begin delegating. Who cares if your husband brings home a dozen eggs and five of them are broken? You are going to break the eggs anyway when you use them. If he comes home with broken eggs, show them to him and let him know that you have done this before yourself and that you quickly learned to open the container and check the eggs in the store to make sure none were cracked before buying them. Instead of belittling him, starting an argument, or putting him down, you are relating to him. If you need the eggs right away, you can always ask him to go back to the store to buy more. Trust me, the first time he has to go out twice for eggs, he will never do it again.

Be patient. You will have to teach anyone you delegate tasks to. Besides, at one point you had to learn those skills too. Give your loved ones and others time to learn how to complete the tasks you delegate to them. Part of learning to be a SuperWoman is not setting your expectations for perfection. You might have to teach your spouse, child, or friend what to do the first few times, but then after a while things will get easier as they help you carry the weight. Teaching takes time initially, but once the lesson is learned, you will find more time for yourself and become more comfortable delegating. Most people who are supporting you want to help you and may even find contentment and fulfillment in being able to give you a hand here and there. Remember, as you release control of other people or the insignificant tasks in your life, you are refocusing and opening up more free time to focus on what's most important to you. And as you let go, you will begin to find more fulfillment and peace.

Mentoring Versus Controlling Children

When it comes to children, I understand that it is hard not to be in control. We have lived through what they are currently going through and we are aware of the outcomes, consequences, and pains they will face. We sometimes control to protect. The reality is that parenting and controlling are two different things. That line can be grey, but growing up and making mistakes is part of everyone's journey. You can protect and guide your adolescents, but ultimately they will have to make their own choices. If your child makes a poor choice, that is not a direct reflection on you. Poor choices and consequences are a reflection of the trials of life.

I'm not suggesting that you don't mentor or discipline your children to prevent them from taking a wrong course that could negatively impact their future. But you do have to understand that adolescents are searching for their identities, have hormonal changes, and often think that they are right. Even the best-behaved teenagers are going through physical and mental challenges.

Think back to when you were a teenager. Sure, it was wonderful not having a mortgage payment or having to work 40 plus hours per week, but it also wasn't easy. Maybe you didn't have bills, but you had gossip, grades, and guys—all of which are troubling. You had to try and fit in and still listen to your parents. You had to figure things out for the first time, like menstruation, cramps, and PE class. Plus, when you were younger you didn't understand a lot, even though you thought you did. It's really not an easy time of life.

We can't change biology. Instead of trying to change and control something you can't, work with what you can control. If you are overly pushy and demanding, you risk your adolescent turning to friends instead of you for advice, running from problems, or engaging in activities that are the opposite of what you want for them.

Try guiding and mentoring instead. You can do this by using empathy or encouraging your teenagers to take control over situations in their life. If adolescents are fighting with friends, chances are they are handing power over to their peers. You may notice them saying things like "She didn't invite me to that party of hers" or "I don't even know why Jennifer is mad at me." Those types of statements demonstrate that the teenager is putting himself or herself into a more passive role or taking on a victim stance.

Rather than lecturing adolescents on how you acted and did things when you were a teenager, make your help all about them. Educate them on getting back the power they relinquished to their peers. Teach your son to speak up. Advise him to ask his friend directly if he can come to the party or ask his friend why he wasn't invited. If your daughter doesn't know why Jennifer is mad at her, encourage her to ask Jennifer why she is upset. Jennifer is probably upset about a rumor or something that might not have even taken place, and this conversation will give your daughter the opportunity to clear the air.

Despite the fact that you have been through these scenarios before and these issues seem really small to you now, recognize that this is your adolescent's first time going through these types of situations. They don't care what you did when you were a teenager. To them, times have changed, you are ancient, and they are going through it right now. Try to remember how you felt fighting with your first boyfriend or with your girlfriends. Then empathize with your daughter. Perhaps you can help her make a list of "10 reasons why boyfriends suck." Find out what her likes are and what is important in her world and work with those concepts. Changing your reactions toward your children will change how they react toward you, and you may even educate them along the way.

WHY WE FEEL THE NEED TO CONTROL

Control can also become a big issue in relationships where women try to change and control men. Women assume that if they can maintain control over certain aspects of their partner, there will be less of the unknown to fear and at some point "he will come around." Women rationalize this behavior by saying, "I'm not controlling him, I'm just guiding him." Wrong! When you take your key and try to control someone else's car with it, you are setting yourself up for disappointment as well as a potential crash.

People have to want to change, and they can't just say that they want to change. They have to really want to and believe that they can. You can lead a horse to water, but you can't make him drink, as the saying goes. You increase your likelihood of disappointment and reduce your personal fulfillment the more you try to change someone.

Another issue that arises when we try to change someone and can't is that, as women, we tend to hold ourselves very accountable when we fail at something. That increases our self-doubt, decreases our confidence, and potentially increases symptoms of depression. The more we realize that we have wasted our energy and time on someone or something that did not change, the longer we cycle around the Ferris wheel with regret.

What's also unhealthy about this kind of behavior is that patterns of repeated negativity get your brain into the habit of observing more failures as opposed to successes. When you try to change someone but they never change or they constantly revert back to their old ways, you begin to internalize their failure. If you are trying to teach them a lesson and, again and again, your efforts are not working, you think "I must be doing something wrong." Essentially you are taking on their failure too. Those repeated failures negatively skew your confidence and focus your mind on failures. What's the way out of that cycle? *Stop trying to control other people. Let them take control of themselves.* That way if they fail, they fail—not you. Take the weight of controlling others off of yourself and give it back to them.

Some women have so little control over their own lives that they cling to those who need control or who seem to be inviting control into their lives. One example is the woman who seeks out the "bad boy." Bad boys need to be tamed or controlled, and a woman who lacks the ability to control her own life is up for the challenge. A woman who pursues the bad boy as her challenge may even find herself taking on the motherly role as she tries to mend and mold him. But trying to mend, mold, and change someone is taking on an entirely new life role—a huge commitment of time and energy.

As I said, people need to have control. In fact, control is an essential part of our lives. The problem is, if for whatever reason you do not have good control over your own life, your mind still wants some control. So your mind tries to find other people or things it might be able to control in order to release this desire. Think for a moment about small children. They have no control or very limited control over what they do, what they eat, etc. Besides, at three years old what can you really control in this big world? Ah ha, your toys! That is why children are so possessive of their toys— how to play with them and where to put them. For that reason, it's best not to touch children's toys. Let them have that control.

Another element in the control dynamic is that women who have abusive or controlling partners may feel that they have been robbed of their personal self-control. If control has been taken away from us in some way, we may seek control through other avenues. In a situation where a woman is in an abusive and controlling relationship, she may find herself overbearing with her children to compensate for the lack of control within herself and her marriage. Women with eating disorders also tend to lack control in their lives. Research shows that women who are anorexic perceive that they have minimal control over their lives. The one thing they see that they can control is their food intake and weight.

Does any of this sound familiar to you? If so, does your need to control come down to fear—perhaps a fear of losing something or someone? Do you lack control in yourself and are you trying to regain it by controlling others? Regardless of the reason you seek control, take time to search for the answer within yourself. The self-reflection process can be painful and eye opening, but self-awareness can mean self-fulfillment.

Once you are aware of your fears or the reasons why you feel the need to control others, you can begin to focus back on yourself. If you recognize fear as a barrier in your life, instead of trying to control others as a fix, identify your fears so that you can begin putting in place a plan to work over and around this barrier. Identifying fears and putting a plan in place to work through your pain moves you one step closer to taking back control.

Is Anxiety Hiding under Your Anger?

Another major barrier to women's fulfillment that I've observed in my work is anger. Anger is poison. It makes us do and say stupid things that we later regret. When we hold on to anger, we end up hurting ourselves. If you are mad at someone, how are you hurting *them* by sitting around and brewing day in and day out about how much *you* are angry? They are going about their lives, taking the opportunities that come their way, and living in the moment while you sit there spending your energy on them.

The real way to "get back" at someone is to channel your anger into something you love and do it! You will be so consumed with life that you'll be better able to put into perspective what really matters to you. If you are angry because you think someone is making your life miserable, it's only because you are letting them. They have one key and it goes to their car. Do not allow them to put their key into your vehicle and drive it.

Anger is a mixed emotion. Some people who are angry may go to see a therapist for help, but no matter how many times they are taught and use anger-management techniques, they don't get better. That's because the actual problem for them is anxiety not anger. The anger is masking their anxiety, and until the anxiety is minimized, the anger will never really go down.

I was once counseling a family where the parents were in the middle of a divorce. In one session, we processed the divorce and the adolescent boy took the news extremely well. That was in June. As the holidays were approaching, I noticed a change in this very smart and well-behaved boy. He began cursing, getting upset at his mother, and randomly having bouts of tears because he wasn't seeing his father as much. He became very rude toward his sister. His behavior also changed in school and he started acting out. He was riddled with anger.

I tried various anger-management techniques and they helped for the short term only. While on the outside the issue appeared to be anger, I quickly realized that this boy's anger was masking his anxiety. I decided to take a different approach and use techniques to help him talk about what might be causing him to feel anxious. At first he denied that he was anxious at all. As time went on, though, the boy talked about the pain he felt because he would not be with both his parents during the holidays. He wanted more clarity about how visitations would work. His anxiety about the unknown and about his upcoming life experiences needed to be addressed in order for the anger to subside.

Whenever you notice yourself or others becoming more and more angry, look below the surface to see if the anger is masking an underlying problem of anxiety. If you can identify what stressors you have in life and tackle those problems first, you will notice your anger going down too. Say you are angry with your sister because she doesn't help out with your sick mother. You can't change your sister, but you can change your actions and your reactions to your sister and your mother about the situation.

Identify specifically what might be causing you stress and anxiety about your sister. Maybe you are really feeling "I never have time to work out because I am tending to my mother." Because the real cause of your stress is not being able to work out, your anger won't go away unless you start working out—even if your sister were to start helping. And if you don't solve the real problem, you might shift your anger onto someone else should your sister begin to help care for your mother.

Once you identify the root stressors in your life, you can begin to create a plan to minimize them. In the example above, your goal would no longer be "to get my sister to help out with my sick mom" but rather "I will go over to my mother's house and help her only after I get my morning workout completed."

Self-awareness is key in dealing with barriers of anger and anxiety. If you have emotional pain, you cannot start to deal with the pain unless you are aware of the real issues at play. You have to take time to reflect on the root cause of your pain. That doesn't necessarily mean you have to talk about your childhood for years on end, but it does mean you need to take time to self-reflect and understand what pain you are actually feeling. You do not want to misdiagnosis your pain or mistreat it. Doing so is a waste of your time and energy, and you risk losing confidence in yourself. (The second activity at the end of this chapter will give you the opportunity to uncover your real stressors and create a plan to address them.)

Learn to Compartmentalize

Another way that anger can mask the real issues we need to deal with is that by getting angry, we take the blame off of ourselves. Anger not only assists us in finding fault in others, but it also eliminates or minimizes the responsibility we should be taking upon ourselves. In essence, we hide behind our anger.

Blame or anger toward others may also be a way of minimizing the chances that our insecurities will surface. Some of us want to hide our insecurities because if we allow them to show up, we risk people seeing that we are not who we say we are, and that creates anxiety. By getting angry, we are, in effect, attempting to direct the attention off of ourselves and onto someone or something else.

Placing blame onto someone or something else and away from the real source of our pain is called displacement. Displacement is a defense mechanism for alleviating anxiety when we are faced with aggression or anger. An example of displacement is when you come home after being yelled at by your boss and you scream at your husband. You're not mad at your husband; you're just taking out on your husband the anxiety and anger that your boss provoked.

One way around the tendency to displace our anger onto others is to work at what I call compartmentalizing problems. Compartmentalizing problems or issues means to keep your emotions and problems in the area in which they are troubling you. If you are mad at your boss and you compartmentalize, you keep your angry emotions in the work area of your life. That doesn't mean you should walk into work being mad but that you don't let your anger from work spill into a different compartment of your life, such as the marriage compartment. You can talk to your spouse about how upset you are with your boss, but if your husband has tried to make a nice dinner for you but burned it, don't suddenly lash out at him, bringing up problems from five years ago. A burnt dinner doesn't justify an entire night's fight, especially if he was trying to do something special for you. If you fight all night over the burnt dinner, it's likely that some of the anger from the work compartment is spilling over into the marriage compartment. Now, instead of work being the primary problem, you have created an additional, unnecessary problem with your spouse.

When you compartmentalize your problems, you are able to experience a bad day at work, come home, and turn to your spouse for support as opposed to displacing your anger onto him. Keep your negative emotions in their own compartment and don't penalize people who have nothing to do with the real frustrations you are feeling.

This method of compartmentalizing goes for larger issues as well. Do not make the people in your life who were not present in the past responsible for your past. Compartmentalize the people who hurt you in the past and leave them in their own compartment. Do not hurt a loved one who is undeserving of that pain, and do not sabotage a relationship with someone who could be a loving and healthy support for you.

If you were hurt in the past by a lover, it's not fair to make your new lover suffer by taking out your old angers on him. If an old lover cheated on you, it doesn't mean your new lover is going to. I know that you have pain and insecurities because of what previously happened to you, but realize that these are two different people who probably don't even know each other and who have completely different backgrounds. Your insecurities need to stay in the "old lover" compartment so you don't ruin a potentially great new relationship.

It's hard to get over doubts and insecurities, but if you can consistently look at how the two compartments of "old lover" and "new lover" are different, this will help make you look at your current situation more realistically. In fact, you can take a piece of paper and on one side write your old lover's name and on the other side write your new lover's name. Under each name, write that person's characteristics or things that that person did or did not do for you. This will visually show you how different those two compartments are and why one person should not be blamed for another person's mistakes.

Displacing your anger at one person onto someone else can be the root of much discontent and unhappiness for you and for those you are in a relationship with. If you are unhappy now, you may be giving someone permission to make you feel that way or you could be feeling the effects of hurting those who are a part of your major life roles even though they are undeserving of this pain. You want the people within your top five life roles to be happy and strong. If they are not, start by checking to make sure that you are not displacing unnecessary emotions or pain onto them, whether it's anxiety, anger, insecurity, or something else.

Anxiety and anger sometimes seem like unstoppable barriers. As women, we can have anxiety over a variety of things. It's important to evaluate your anger and anxieties to determine if some of these emotions stem from hidden insecurities. If that is the case, ask yourself: *What can I do to alter or address these insecurities? What issues can I compartmentalize?*

As you explore what you might be insecure or anxious about in certain areas of your life, take time to reflect and journal on these issues. Remember, you cannot change the person or circumstance you are mad at or that is triggering the feeling of uncertainty. You have to change yourself. That means changing your actions and reactions to people and situations that arise. You have one key and you can only drive your own car.

HONESTY IS KEY

I've designed this chapter to help you become more aware of the real barriers or issues that hinder your growth, fulfillment, and relationships. Now it's time to get specific as you identify the barriers that might be stopping you from seeking higher fulfillment.

For any goal you ever want to achieve in life, expect barriers along the way. That is normal. All of us, SuperWomen included, have our challenges to face. Barriers are a part of the process of success and fulfillment. Life consistently throws twists and turns at us. We need to mend, mold, and change our course of action to hurdle the barrier. Accept that barriers do occur, but once a barrier has popped up, make sure you identify it. To identify personal barriers, you'll need to engage in self-reflection. Once you're aware of what is stopping you from being more fulfilled, you can develop your plan to work through the barriers, propelling yourself toward a better work-life balance.

In the beginning of this book, I said that you were going to embark on a journey toward finding fulfillment. That is exactly what this is—a journey. You will not find "you" until you are authentic with yourself and discover the root of your pain or nonfulfillment and the barriers that are holding you back.

Keep in mind as you think about your barriers that sometimes we ourselves are a barrier to our own fulfillment. Many of us are not honest about our barriers. Perhaps your integrity is on the line because of something you did and you don't want to admit that that is a barrier. I have counseled married women who have been unfaithful and are suffering from a lack of fulfillment. Being unfaithful takes time and energy and can therefore be a barrier. You have to be honest and account for this when reflecting on your life and your barriers. Other women find themselves doing something unlawful or unethical, and they must account for the pain, time, and energy that go into those activities. Others hold grudges or hang on to the past in an unhealthy way. Be sure that you also list those types of barriers in the important activity named "What Stops Me from Pursuing My Fulfillment" below. You have to live in line with your personal values to really feel that you have life fulfillment.

To peel off the layers of your personal self and find what your core self needs and desires, honesty is key. If you do not plan to complete your reflections in an authentic and honest manner, you are not yet ready to move forward.

As you explore your inner self and get in touch with your true emotions, you will get to know yourself better. You may also find activities that excite you, relax you, or even scare you. Your journey toward fulfillment will be eye-opening and sometimes hard to face. But the more authentic you are with yourself, the more solutions, possibilities, and plans for fulfillment you'll be able to come up with.

~

Peace is a daily, a weekly, a monthly process,
gradually changing opinions, slowly eroding old barriers,
quietly building new structures.

—JOHN F. KENNEDY

CHANGING MY REACTIONS
VERSUS CONTROLLING

List below some of the people or situations you are trying to control or change that just aren't changing:

1. _____

2. _____

3. _____

Now think outside the box and list at least three techniques you can use to change and control *your* actions or reactions toward these people or situations:

1. _____

_____

2. _____

_____

3. _____

_____

UNCOVERING MY REAL STRESSORS

This three-part activity will help you uncover and address the real stressors in your life. By identifying the real sources of your anxiety, you can create better solutions to minimize those stressors by changing your actions and reactions. First, identify people or areas in your life that you feel most anger you. (For example: *"I am very angry with my sister."*)

1. _____

2. _____

3. _____

Now, identify the real stressors within the areas of life you specified above. (For example: *"I never have time to work out because I am tending to my mother."*)

Root stressor 1._____

Root stressor 2._____

Root stressor 3._____

What are some of the ways can you take action to address the real stressors behind your anger instead of directing anger at others? (For example: *"I will go over to my mother's house and help her only after I get my morning workout completed."*)

1. _____

_____

2. _____

_____

3. _____

_____

WHAT STOPS ME FROM PURSUING MY FULFILLMENT

Being authentic and finding the root of your nonfulfillment can be challenging, but it is part of your journey, so take your time with this activity. Please make sure that you are in an environment where you can be open and honest with yourself. Here are some suggestions that will help you to be authentic as you reflect on what might be hindering your fulfillment:

- As you reflect on your life and experiences, be in a space where you are most comfortable.

- Avoid reflecting amongst distractions in your environment (texting, TV on, children screaming, social media pages open on computer).

- Don't judge yourself.

- Avoid spending your time judging other people and what they should or should not do.

- Don't let other people see the personal reflections you write down. (That way, you can be fully open about who you are.)

- Avoid being biased toward others. Be open to new people and experiences. Stepping out of the same way of thinking can offer you new opportunities and relationships, which in turn can lead to fulfillment.

- Avoid comparing yourself to others.

- Just be honest.

First, create a list of people, fears, situations, ideas, thoughts, etc. that are currently stopping you from pursuing your life balance and fulfillment.

1. _____

2. _____

3. _____

4. _____

5. _____

6. _____

7. _____

8. _____

9. _____

10. _____

....

My Plan for Defeating My Barriers

Now that you are a bit more aware of your barriers and can visually see a list of them, you can devise a plan to work through them. A plan of action will assist you in not being bullied by your barriers and help you avoid being cornered when in an uncomfortable situation. When your barriers try to push you back onto the Ferris wheel, revolving the same old patterns, now you will be more conscious of your choices. You can either pay for another ride around or you can get off the Ferris wheel.

To help you work out a plan, first take each barrier you listed above and identify what is not true about it. Once you can identify what about your barriers isn't actually a real problem, you can begin to work on what is the real issue at hand. Here is an example:

Barrier #1: *I never have enough time.*

What about this barrier is not all true: *"Never" is not really true. I am just busy and feel I can't get a break.*

The next time this barrier rears its ugly head, I plan to do the following: *When I feel overwhelmed and don't think that I have enough time, I am going to look at my schedule and see what I think I have to do that day but don't really have to do. I will also reflect on what I am taking on for the rest of the day or week that I can delegate. I will also take a break from my frustration and go for a 10-minute walk when I am overwhelmed by feeling that I don't have enough time to do everything. I will make time to do what's most important.*

On blank pieces of paper, continue your self-exploration. For each barrier you named under "What Stops Me from Pursuing My Fulfillment," write down the answers to "What about this barrier is not all true?" and "The next time this barrier rears its ugly head, I plan to do the following."

Finally, be sure to follow through. When a barrier pops up, turn back to your written plan for defeating that barrier and take the action you committed to taking. Turning back to your original plan will also spark your mind to recall why you started working toward a specific goal in the first place. It might help to reignite lost passion too. Don't get rid of a goal you're working on because of one barrier. You can always revise your plans as barriers arise and still stay on the right path; but when you leave the path altogether, it's sometimes hard to ever find it again.

SuperWoman Skills

**I identify and work through the real
barriers to my fulfillment.**

A SuperWoman accepts that there will be barriers
on her journey toward success and fulfillment.

A SuperWoman is aware of and understands
what barriers she frequently encounters.

A SuperWoman has a plan to work through her barriers.

A SuperWoman controls her actions and reactions.

A SuperWoman knows that she cannot control others.
She can guide them, but she can't drive their car for them.

A SuperWoman compartmentalizes her frustrations.

A SuperWoman recognizes where her frustrations are
coming from and works not to displace her anger
onto those undeserving of that behavior.

CHAPTER 4

LEARN TO ENJOY
YOUR LIFE

~

You have taken time to reflect on the barriers in your life. You were authentic in defining your barriers and misbeliefs. You even devised an action plan that you feel safe acting upon when the barriers rear their ugly heads. Moving forward, you have two potential problems. First, humans are creatures of habit. People try to change their actions and behaviors but easily revert back to their old ways. Second, when you attempt to implement your plan, you may discover that you feel awkward or uneasy acting on it. Being a creature of habit makes it challenging for any of us to successfully change our behaviors.

The best predictor of future behavior is past behavior, and there is a reason for that statement. We are who we are. It is hard to change ourselves or our habits. In therapy, I talk with women who try to "change" their partners, something

I touched on in the last chapter. I tell them, "It took 35 years to make that man and you cannot make him change his habits in six months!" Women attempt to rationalize their partner's behaviors and work effortlessly to teach him how he "should" be. The man may try to improve his behavior for a few weeks, but he almost always reverts back to the way he was. Reverting back to old behaviors is not something only men do; it's a human issue.

If you want to move forward, you really have to want to move forward. If you want to discover a new you, you have to make a conscious effort with every breath you take. You have to be highly conscious and aware of all your interactions and experiences during the day in order to be more effective and fulfilled.

You have to be aware of your behaviors and reactions because your focus is now on moving forward and not returning to old habits. If you step away from awareness of the self for just one decision, you may find yourself on one more trip around the Ferris wheel. You also have to be sure to drop a role in order to devote yourself to your new role. That new role is focusing on you. Doing that isn't easy because of our deeply ingrained patterns of behavior. In this chapter, you'll learn about developing an indispensable habit that will help you focus on yourself—the habit of getting comfortable being comfortable.

How Stress Wears Us Down

Women spend a lot of time being uncomfortable, perhaps to avoid feelings of guilt or the fear that we might lose someone if we focus on ourselves. Women are overwhelmed and face anxiety and stressors every day. Depression is also common in women. Whether the depression is caused by hormonal issues or lack of fulfillment, 25 percent of women will experience depression in their lifetime and only one in five will seek any type of treatment. Women aged 40 to 60 are under the most stress. Research shows that women in this group face frequent and consistent stress, which comes with its own set of problems.

Consistent and chronic stress is detrimental to the body, both mentally and physically. When the body faces a stressor, cortisol, adrenaline, and other hormones are released into the body. The release of these chemicals is a way for your body to protect itself. This gives you a boost when you really need to react with fight or flight. There have been stories of people lifting cars off the ground to save their children from a burning vehicle. The boost of adrenaline and hormones puts the body into a sometimes unreal state so it can get through an attack. When the fight is over, the body recovers and our hormones go back to their appropriate levels.

For women who are faced with living in a fight-or-flight state every day because of multiple stressors, the amount of cortisol and other hormones does not drop back to appropriate levels. Hormones remain unbalanced because the body thinks it needs to be in a fight-or-flight state all the time. Overexposure to these hormones can lead to anxiety, heart disease, stomach-related issues, sleep problems, depression, weight changes, and memory issues.

Another health issue that arises for women is that because we typically nurture and take care of others when we are ill, we attempt to heal ourselves without any outside help when we become sick. The truth is that when you are feeling sick, you might not know what is really wrong with you. Your illness could be psychosomatic or it could be physical. Panic attacks and heart attacks share several of the same symptoms. You might think you can treat your own panic attack but, for sure, you can't treat your own heart attack. Heart disease is the leading cause of death among women, and two-thirds of women will not make a full recovery after having a heart attack.

I said earlier that women are strong and often do have the right answers, but for everyone else. When it comes to ourselves, we ignore the answers and sometimes we don't even know the questions we should ask. A SuperWoman knows how important it is to get support. When you are down, whether it's physically or emotionally, call upon your family or professional supports. I understand that you might fear disappointing your family or co-workers, but relationships are 50-50. When you are down, you need to be sure that you give yourself the same time and attention you would give to others. Even more challenging, you have to work on not feeling guilty once you do ask for help from your support systems.

A 50-50 relationship does not mean that on Monday mornings you carry the weight and then Monday evenings your spouse carries the weight. It means that there might be months where you are head of the household and then your spouse picks up that role later in life. For example, if your spouse gets in an accident at work, you may be responsible for carrying more responsibility than you normally do. But when he heals, it's his turn to help out and allow you to focus on yourself. When it's time for you to find fulfillment, your partner needs to pick up his 50 percent.

Be cognizant of self-defeating thoughts that trick you into believing that those who are your supports won't help you work toward fulfillment. Do not let self-defeating thoughts become a habitual barrier for you and be sure to eliminate faulty thinking that won't allow you to see your situation from a different angle. Use your strengths. Use your confidence as an aggressive way to seek fulfillment and use your communal nature to rally up support systems when you are down.

Prevention and the Mind-Body Connection

We come from a society where health care has always been focused on fixing the problem. As SuperWomen, we need to change our own mindset to prevention. Don't let a problem start; prevent it from ever happening. You may initially feel that you are going to the doctor more frequently, but the visits will be more positive and, in the long run, less financially and emotionally expensive. Forget the saying "Don't fix it unless it's broke" and adopt the motto "Fix it, update it, and take care of it before it breaks."

Some women will go for days or weeks on end being ill, downing over-the-counter medication until their body shuts down completely. After harassment from family and friends, they visit the doctor, only to find that they have pneumonia or some other serious condition. My mother-in-law had chest pain, jaw pain, and shortness of breath and still waited to see a doctor. She is strong. She raised a family, went through pain of different sorts her whole life, and made it through. Her habit of taking care of others encouraged her to feel that she could take care of this pain too. It wasn't until the shortness of breath became unbearable that she decided to go to the doctor. She walked into the doctor's office with shortness of breath and walked out the office door with an immediate date in hand for triple bypass heart surgery!

Research shows that our state of mind affects our state of health. As women, we can face a high level of mental and emotional stress on a consistent basis, which can then quickly wear down our immune systems and make us susceptible to illness. We allow such high amounts of stress in our lives and avoid caring for ourselves because we have conditioned ourselves to be comfortable in our uncomfortable state.

Earlier I mentioned the tendency many of us have to fill up the moments we could be using for a break. When we've completed a project or are waiting for something to come through, instead of taking the couple of hours of downtime for ourselves, God forbid, we fill it with more work. That is because we are actually *comfortable being uncomfortable.* We will find things to do to fill this downtime because we are not comfortable just sitting. When we sit, we discover our thoughts, likes, and dislikes. That can be a great thing, but it can be scary too. Plus, we have guilt that riddles us as we sit there knowing we could be doing so much more for our family or for our jobs.

The reality is, as a "super woman" you have probably taken on a number of roles and life activities and tried to juggle many things at once, which can quickly drain you mentally and physically. As you work toward becoming a SuperWoman, who values work-life balance and personal fulfillment, it's important to be in tune with your body and receive regular health and wellness checkups. Routine check-ups can help us focus on being more proactive as opposed to either ignoring our bodies or being reactive. A SuperWoman knows that her body and mind are her most valuable tools in life and thus she cares for them as much, if not more than, she cares for everyone and everything else.

Allowing Yourself to Enjoy the Moment

When you sit and relax, you are in fact doing a lot for your health and subsequently for your family and career. The healthier and more fulfilled you are, the more time and energy you will have to give to the people or things that mean the most to you. Relaxing, taking space, meditating, or focusing on the present gives us the ability to take in the moment. Taking in the moment is something people pay me to teach them. It's a skill and a goal for women and men alike. You'll benefit greatly by learning to feel comfortable when you are alone. I'm not talking about being alone while you are working, but being alone with yourself. Take time to meditate. Teach your brain to turn off. Can you imagine a moment of silence, let alone a moment of silence when your brain is quiet?

I have a canal in the back of my yard. The first year I moved to my home, I took it for granted. I loved looking at the canal, but I never experienced it. The second year, I decided to get a kayak. I decided that time for me was necessary and I was really lucky to have this as my backyard. I needed to practice what I had preached. I no longer wanted to take this beautiful waterway for granted and I also wanted to enjoy more moments.

I don't take hour-long kayak rides during the week because I do have priorities and my work, but I use the waterway to experience life every so often for 20 minutes. I kayak for about 10 minutes and then sit. There is dead silence and the sun is looking down on me. When my mind trails off to work, I tell myself that for these 20 minutes I am all that matters. I cannot change anything at that moment. That moment will make me stronger in the moments that lie ahead of me that day. Earlier you read about the importance of being in the moment with a child or spouse when you are giving time to that particular life role. Now you know that focusing on yourself is a life role too. So when you are alone with yourself, focus on yourself. Answering your boss's call while "in the moment" does not count as "you time."

Men are really good at keeping a divide between work and life. They do not let less-important tasks interfere with their ability to have a life. If the laundry does not get done for a week, they are still assured that the sky will not fall upon them. Men don't care if they look fat in jeans and they don't have a mild heart attack when the baby bumps into the table. They fight with friends and are over it in five minutes, and they don't sweat a lot of the small stuff. They are happy fishing. Fishing is an activity where they stare at water with a pole in their hands for hours on end, often reeling up an empty line.

Men can also turn emotions on and off quickly and they avoid holding grudges. If we tell our partners about a co-worker who is treating us poorly, they give us a solution and expect us to march on. Then we get mad at them. Reality check: men are actually right in these situations. We should look for more solutions and avoid holding long emotional grudges. Chances are, if the baby tumbles, he will be just fine and you probably do not look fat in those jeans. And staring at the water with a fishing pole in hand for hours might just mean that men know how to enjoy the moment.

Keep this in mind too: the less time you take to focus on the moment, the greater your chances for depression. In addition, research suggests that people who are depressed are more prone to having their brains pick up more negative statements and comments than those who do not have depression. Negativity brews negativity.

During my coaching sessions and SuperWoman workshops, I invite clients and participants to play what I like to call the "brain game." I take a bowl of cooked pasta noodles and set it aside. I ask the client to come up with her own positive and negative statement cards about herself. Then we put the positive and negative statement cards into a bucket.

I ask the client to pull out each card during the course of the activity, but only one at a time. When she pulls out a positive statement card, she gets an inspirational card to read and take home. When she pulls out a negative card, I ask her to pour a dark-colored spice onto the clean noodles, representing her brain. By the end of the game, the client is able to see how negative thoughts, one at a time, even when added slowly, will consume her brain. How can we set goals, meet goals, and have healthy support systems when our entire brain is consumed with negative thoughts? We can't.

Your Body Needs Time to Rejuvenate

Another element of self-care that women neglect is their sleep. Lack of sleep can also impact fulfillment and increase feelings of depression or anxiety. Having your sleep broken up is painful. The body only really rests and rejuvenates tissues in REM (rapid eye movement) sleep. REM sleep is the sleep stage where we dream. In REM sleep, the body systems and brain are hard at work rejuvenating while the muscles of the body go into a paralyzed state. We typically move into REM sleep 90 minutes after we have fallen asleep, and then move in and out of REM sleep throughout the night.

Have you ever slept for eight hours and woken up tired or not refreshed and then at other times slept for five hours and felt great? That is because if you sleep eight, ten, twelve hours but you do not get REM sleep or do not spend enough time in REM sleep, your body and tissues have not fully rested. Your body needs time to rejuvenate. If you sleep for five hours but most of that sleep is deep sleep, you tend to feel more rested than if you had more hours of sleep that was interrupted.

Some women indicate that they cannot exercise because of time constraints. However, the more you work out, the more quickly your body is able to pull you into REM sleep. For every 30 minutes you work out, your body can pull you into REM sleep 60 minutes sooner. This theory caps out at one hour of working out. If you work out for one hour, your body can pull you into REM sleep two hours earlier. This means that you can net up to an extra hour per day to do whatever you want. If you choose to take that extra time and spend it on work versus life, that is your choice. But I encourage you to become comfortable taking this extra time for your personal fulfillment.

Since women are caregivers by nature, we are comfortable lying in bed staring at the ceiling while everyone else is asleep. We might even get up to clean at midnight or write a book. If our children are ill, we pray to take over the flu for them. I have even talked with women clients who sacrifice going to the doctor to save on a co-pay or deductible. That is no way to live. Your family, career, and the people in your top life roles need you and they need you healthy. *You* need you healthy.

Freeing Up Your Time and Energy

When I work with women clients, I typically begin the first couple coaching sessions exploring their values and mission statements for their lives. This gets them in the mode of focusing on themselves. For some women, this process is very challenging because it is a rarity for them to spend even one hour focusing only on themselves.

Rather than being comfortable with what's uncomfortable, your upcoming challenge is to *be comfortable being comfortable*. That means being overworked, overspoused, overstressed, and stepped over will actually be over.

If you feel you are *overworked*, reflect on what you could delegate or what don't have to do. Delegating or minimizing your "haves-to-dos" will free up time for you to begin focusing more on yourself. If you feel that you are *overspoused,* begin to find ways to speak up and talk with your partner. It's not always easy to speak up to a spouse for a variety of reasons. However, the more you do it, the more proficient you will become at asking for what you need. If you are *overstressed*, take some time to review your stressors, which you reflected on in chapter 3. One by one, go down the list and see where you can change your response to others to reduce stress. Review the list to see where you can set more boundaries. Review the list to see where you might be acting out of line with your morals and values. Then implement the changes that are necessary to free up time and energy.

Changing your responses to people, setting boundaries, delegating, and speaking up are all factors that might make you feel uncomfortable at times. However, the more you engage in these behaviors, the more comfortable you'll start feeling with what was once uncomfortable for you. When you implement change or let go of past issues or responsibilities that you don't have to take on, you will discover that you have more time to focus on yourself and your fulfillment.

If you spend time worrying about the future and complaining about your past, you have no time to enjoy life in the present. One quote I chuckle at every time I think of it is "Complaining about complaining is still complaining." Grab a notebook and every time you have fear or guilt or dwell on the past, put a little tally mark on the paper. At the end of the day, look at how much time you have spent doing those activities. Wouldn't you rather spend your life doing something else?

There is all this debate over nature versus nurture. Is it my biological makeup or it is the way my family treated me? These concepts do play a role in who we are, but why blame nature or nurture or why spend your time trying to figure out which one made you ride the Ferris wheel? Quit blaming, take responsibility, and focus on yourself. The more you focus on yourself and your needs, the more you will find that you are quite comfortable being comfortable.

REWARD YOURSELF

Reverting back to old habits is easy. Remaining comfortable being uncomfortable may seem easiest in the short run because you are used to that way of living. In the long run, however, it can be very detrimental to your health and life fulfillment. To change your habits, you will not only need a plan for how to have a more fulfilling life, but you will also have to set up a reward system for yourself. Whenever you travel outside of your comfort zone, whenever you take a risk, whenever you reach out for support, you get a reward.

At first these behaviors will feel awkward, but that is good because the way you have been living has not provided you with all the fulfillment you desire and deserve. A true SuperWoman will reward herself for traveling outside of her comfort zone and will not feel guilty—because she recognizes she has earned it.

Reward yourself all the time, several times per day. I do not necessarily mean that you should get five lattes, a pedicure, and a massage every day. Reward yourself with something small but fun. For example, if you take the stairs instead of the elevator, you get to eat that Hershey Kiss sitting on your desk (I won't tell). If you work out an extra five minutes, you can hit that bookstore you love for ten minutes before going home. If you are extra helpful to someone, tell the coffee shop *not* to hold the whip cream this time.

I notice that a lot of the women I counsel want to increase how much water they drink. Together, we work to cut out the sodas and introduce more water. Water lubricates joints and moistens body tissues. It gives the body a better overall feeling. When the women I work with reach their daily goal for water intake, they reward themselves with something small. Even tea or a cup of coffee in between water intake suffices as a reward. This process is about doing work but rewarding yourself with small bits of life.

Think rewards every day, all day. This will get you into a habit of focusing on things you like. It will also help you begin to navigate away from being comfortable with what's uncomfortable and move toward feeling comfortable being comfortable.

What happens if you complete a larger goal in your life? The small daily goals are goals like drinking water, exercising, and saying no to someone you always say yes to. But what if you met all your sales goals at work for the quarter? What if you applied for that MBA and got accepted into the program? Reward yourself big time! These goals are no small feat. Celebrate. But what can you give yourself? Well, it should be something more than that little Hershey Kiss, but probably not a brand-new Mercedes each time.

For the bigger rewards, I recommend that you make a bucket list. Your bucket list should include leisure activities as well as desired lifetime achievements and professional goals. Perhaps getting into an MBA program was both a goal you achieved and a bucket list item. That's okay. To reward yourself for achieving your goal, you pull out your bucket list to search for something leisure-related and do it. It could be "try paddle boarding," "swim with the dolphins," or "go on a cruise to the Bahamas."

Bucket list rewards do not necessarily have to be expensive and larger than life. They can be things you want to experience in life before you kick the can, things that will add meaning and fulfillment to your life as a whole. When you reach a major goal and plan to reward yourself with something off the bucket list, think about getting others involved. Doing something for yourself while also having family or friends share in it with you will reduce feelings of guilt and foster more love and support.

Use the bucket list form below to begin to list all the activities in life you ever wanted to do or take part in. I recommend that you list 100 activities. I encourage you to mark off at least four bucket list items per year. The bucket list form is not easy to fill out. We all have our top 10 "kick the can" to dos, but to list 100 takes some self-exploration. If you have old journals or diaries from when you were younger, take those out and review them. This will help you connect with your inner child and reflect on what you had always hoped you would do or would become. Talk to friends, flip through magazines, sit in a park, or look at old photo albums to help inspire you or assist you in remembering what you wanted out of life.

Working on your bucket list and learning to reward yourself consistently in big and little ways are all part of re-training yourself to be comfortable enjoying life as you strive for fulfillment. You don't have go through life being uncomfortable or unfulfilled. Allow yourself to put the life back into work-life balance—and have some fun doing it.

∼

We first make our habits,
and then our habits make us.

—JOHN DRYDEN

My Bucket List

The purpose of the worksheet that follows is to get you to think about all the things you want to experience and do before you "kick the can." Think about both career *and* personal goals you have. Here are a couple of rules for the bucket list:

- Every single bucket list item cannot be to travel somewhere. I am sure we all have 100 different islands we want to go to before we kick the can, but listing 100 different destinations to visit is not the point of this activity. Plus, going to four different islands a year would be very time consuming and expensive!

- Every single bucket list item can't be work related. The goal of this exercise is to find life fulfillment. If you want to speak at a conference, write a book, or get promoted to CEO, write that down on your bucket list, but also explore life goals you have that are not related to work. You are seeking balance.

On the spaces below, start to create a list of 100 things you will do before you die. You must come up with 10 items today and 20 within one week. Complete the entire list of 100 before the next month's end. Accept the challenge to complete at least a minimum of four of your bucket list items per year.

1. _____

2. _____

3. _____

4. _____

5. _____

6. _____

7. _____

8. _____

9. _____

10. _____

Continue creating your list of 100 activities in your journal, on a separate piece of paper, or on the downloadable form at www.mindfulrehab.com under "SuperWoman Worksheets."

SuperWoman Skills

I enjoy my life.

A SuperWoman is comfortable being comfortable.

A SuperWomen changes her mindset toward prevention.

A SuperWoman knows that her body and mind
are her most valuable tools in life and cares for them.

A SuperWoman rewards herself every day.

A SuperWoman works toward fulfilling
her own bucket list.

CHAPTER 5

SET SMART GOALS

∾

Get a grip! I mean, get a goal. Goals are important to have because they help us work toward fulfillment. Without strong goals, we assume that cleaning the house or making it through the work week is our goal. Making it through the week is important, but those types of tasks are more like routine to-dos.

We all have to-dos. In fact, we have to have to-dos. They keep us organized and on track. However, don't confuse your to-dos with longer-term life goals meant to personally fulfill you. A clean house may bring an immediate sense of satisfaction, but it doesn't lead to life fulfillment. It's very important to know the difference between a to-do and a goal. In short, to-dos keep us on the Ferris wheel and goals get us off.

One theory as to why goal setting is effective is that when we set goals, there is a discrepancy between what we currently have and what we want. That discrepancy causes a sense of dissatisfaction and our brain has intrusive thoughts about the unfulfilled goal until we have achieved it. We attempt to respond to the discrepancy by working toward our goal. In effect, our dissatisfaction with our current state creates an incentive for us to try and change our situation.

Five Qualities of Good Goals

Thinking or verbalizing your goals is not enough. Goal setting is an art. It takes self-reflection and time to create effective goals. If you have not reached your goals in the past, reflect on the potential reasons why. It can often be the case that we don't meet our goals because they fail the "SMART" test.

Think about the acronym SMART when setting your goals. SMART stands for *specific, measureable, attainable, relevant,* and *time-bound.* If your goal is too broad, you are setting yourself up for failure. If, for instance, my goal is "to take over the world," it wouldn't be *specific* enough to be achievable. What do I want to take over in the world? That goal is also not *measureable.* At what point would I know when I have taken over the world? That goal is also not *attainable* or realistic. With all the security in place in the world and with people having control over their own lives, I will most likely not be able to "take over the world." Taking over the world also isn't *relevant* because it's not in line with my values or path in life. It also doesn't have a clear *time frame* associated with it.

In contrast to that goal, here's an example of a smart (SMART) goal—one that is specific, measureable, and attainable. Say my goal is to finalize the manuscript for another book a year from now. That's *specific*—it states what I want to do. I can *measure* when it is completed based on whether I've written all the chapters and had them edited and proofed. Looking at my life, I have decided that this goal is also *attainable* for me. If I wanted to complete my book in one week, that would not be attainable for me because I cannot commit to the amount of time it would take to write a book in one week. Some people say they can write a book in a week, but I'm not comparing myself to them. Based on my life and what I know I can do and will stick to, my timeline of a year is attainable. This goal is also *relevant* because it is in line with my mission and path in life. It is *time-bound* since I'm giving myself one year to meet this goal.

If you do not set specific, measureable, and attainable goals, you add more barriers to the road you are walking down. You are already going to encounter bumps on your journey toward success. Don't add to that by creating unnecessary barriers from the beginning. Start out your journey on a strong, clear, and focused path. That will increase your confidence and keep you pushing toward your goals when times get rough.

Another block to achieving our goals and to finding fulfillment comes when we set unrealistic expectations for ourselves and compare ourselves to others. If your goal in life is to go back to school and get your master's degree, you cannot look at the time and energy a friend put into her schooling and use that as your marker for success. Look only at your own life when setting goals. Review your barriers and time constraints. Do you have children? Do you have a full-time job? Is this your first time back in school after 10 years? Your circumstances are different from everyone else's. We all have different journeys through life. Give yourself realistic deadlines and milestones so that you do not get discouraged and quit.

You can also decrease your chances of being successful when you create goals that are focused on what others want, not what you truly want, or when you set goals that are based on perfectionism, which makes the goal essentially unattainable. (You'll learn more about the issues associated with being a perfectionist in the next chapter on how to measure your goals.)

One of the reasons it's important to set yourself up for success with good goal setting is that, as women, we are tough on ourselves when we don't succeed. Our confidence can be quickly eroded after one or two attempted and unachieved goals. A pattern of striving to achieve but failing is something we take personally and internalize quickly. That results in a lack of confidence that can prevent us from moving forward with future goals, which in turn hinders our fulfillment and increases our chances of depression. In fact, research shows that individuals who are depressed tend to create goals that are less specific. Good goals boost motivation and add importance to our lives and futures. Without clear and specific goals, our future may not seem bright, fulfilling, or worthy.

Overanalyzing, Overdoing, and Overwhelming Yourself

Another rule of thumb for good goal setting is not to overanalyze. I talked about the importance of being honest about the amount of time it will take you to complete a goal as you work on setting your goals. Just as importantly, don't consume yourself with every little detail of the time and energy it will take to complete the goal. Instead, welcome the learning and growth process. If you start looking at how many text books you will have to buy over the course of four years and how many chapters you will have to read each night, and then begin creating scenarios that might not even come to be, that is self-defeating. And self-defeating behavior is a barrier to attaining your goals. Goal setting should be exciting, not stressful.

When you begin working toward a major life goal and are considering what it entails, it's easy to shut down and walk away. If you overwhelm yourself when working with your goals, you'll push yourself into a fight-or-flight state. Don't let the details become a barrier to your success or fulfillment. Once you set a life goal that you know will lead you toward fulfillment, don't give up or give in. March through the barriers or the discomfort of unknowing and realize that you can always adjust your plans and your timelines as you move forward.

Over the years, I've counseled clients who have overwhelmed themselves with tasks, goals, and family matters. These overachievers come into their coaching session with five or six major life goals that they plan to work toward. Committing yourself to too many tasks and goals at once can create anxiety, and some people with high levels of anxiety find themselves having panic attacks.

Panic attacks are unexpected episodes of fear that lead to physical reactions when no danger is apparent. Panic attacks come out of the blue and can feel as if you're having a heart attack or nervous breakdown. You might be walking the dog, cooking dinner, relaxing on the couch, or reading a book when a panic attack suddenly occurs. Why would someone have a panic attack while reading a romance novel? There is no one cause for a panic attack, but they do tend to occur after a build-up of stress and emotions. Your body and mind work together as a strong team, but they can only handle so much negativity and stress.

Think about the following scenario. You are holding a flat plate in the palm of your right hand. In your left hand, you're holding a cup of water. Now pour the water slowly onto the plate. At first, the plate does rather well holding the water. However, as the water fills the plate, you notice that it's harder for you to balance the plate and you begin having doubts that the plate will be able to continue holding the water. Say I ask you to keep pouring more water onto the plate. You know it's not a good idea, but you do it anyway. Suddenly, you have added so much water that the water starts pouring over the edges of the plate. That's what happens when we have a panic attack. If we continue adding too much to our personal plate in life, at some point our emotions will come barreling over the edge.

When we have too much stress in our lives, our minds and bodies must release that stress and a panic attack is one way that happens. Interestingly, women are twice as likely as men to get a panic attack. Women who do experience panic attacks typically have them starting in young adulthood. That makes sense. We begin college, start a career, get married, and have children. Very quickly our life goes from 0 to 60 miles per hour.

PACE YOURSELF

Many of us underestimate the effect that stress has on our body. Each stage of life brings new goals and ventures, and our body needs time to adapt to these changes. Even good stress, called "eustress," can be overwhelming for the body.

Getting promoted or having a child is wonderful and exciting, but it does add a weight to our body that wasn't there before. That's why pacing is important.

Although it's wonderful to have lots of goals, what is not smart is trying to reach all your life goals at once. When you tackle too much at once—piling several professional, academic, and personal goals onto your plate—the sense of being overwhelmed can shut you down, eventually increasing your chances of depression and lack of fulfillment and decreasing your chances of ever reaching your goals. Think about how you narrowed down your list of life roles in chapter 1. If you feel out of balance when taking on more than five life roles, imagine the pain of depression or anxiety that is added to the mix when you are overwhelmed. It's like taking on two extra and unnecessary life roles. If this goes on for too long or with too much intensity, at some point your body will shut down or put you into a panic-attack state.

To prevent this from happening, be sure to pace yourself. Life is a journey. Enjoy it. It's up to you to find little ways to release the pain and stressors that will arise each day. Whether you've had a challenging or a great day, it's often helpful to journal as a healthy way to release emotions. You can do anything that helps you relax and let go, from taking a walk in a beautiful area or meditating to simply sitting on a patio listening to the sounds of nature around you.

STICK TO YOUR PRIORITY GOALS

We all know that life can change quickly, and with those changes can come more goals, more to-dos, and more stressors. A SuperWoman is aware that changes in life are inevitable and thus she prioritizes and keeps in mind her life roles at all times. It might seem that life forces us to take on too much too soon; but if that's your current perception, take a step back from the situation and assess which goals don't have to be a priority for you right now. This will help to minimize your anxiety toward everything that you perceive is on your plate.

Select two or three goals that will help direct your life onto the path you want to steer toward or stay on and work only on those. I usually suggest choosing two goals to strive for at a time. By targeting two goals to work toward, you can generate balance in your life. You're not focused solely on one task, nor are you spread too thin.

We can easily get caught up in feeling overwhelmed before we realize it if we don't take time to evaluate our priorities before taking on new goals and roles. My neighbor's mother, who is about 60 years old, found this out when she came to town to help her son move. She didn't really want to help, but her son and daughter-in-law were expecting a baby and she felt that they needed her support. She took on activities that increased her already-high levels of anxiety and stress. She doesn't like flying, but she flew. Lifting is hard for her, but she lifted boxes anyway.

During her stay, I had the opportunity to talk with her about some of her stressors. She didn't have many stress outlets, didn't like where she currently lived, and was in too much pain to get out of the house for walks. On top of all that, a few weeks before coming to help her son move, she decided to allow a family member to live with her until she got back on her feet.

As we were talking, this woman realized that to decrease her anxiety and depressive symptoms, she needed to begin focusing on herself *before* agreeing to take on new goals. She needed to think about which life roles were a priority for her and focus on those. If supporting her son, daughter-in-law, and grandchild were now going to be a priority, adding on the stress of having another person living with her was not ideal. Changing living arrangements would only add stress, panic, and potential health problems, as she was already finding out. This is why it's important for us to examine and refine our goals regularly. When you know what your focus is, you'll make better decisions when faced with requests you need to turn down and when tempted to take on major new goals.

Achieving a life goal is a big deal. It's not easy and it doesn't happen overnight. Accomplishing something on your to-do list can happen overnight. I can clean the house in one day, I can complete a project for work in one day, I can exercise in one day. I can't get an MBA, write a book, or change all of my negative habits in one day. Achieving self-improvement and life goals takes a long time. That's why life is called a journey and not a two-day vacation.

Look at your journey as a climb. Every day, as long as you are trying, you are moving up. Even when you hit a bump or think you are moving backwards, you are still climbing up. Be patient with yourself. Patience is a skill; lack of patience is a barrier.

In actuality, fulfillment begins with the first step of your journey and continues to grow as you choose healthy paths for yourself. What I mean by that is it's not only the attainment of the goal that will bring you satisfaction but the path to getting there. Life fulfillment is going to creep up on you during your journey toward your goal. Your personal goal might be to start your own business or obtain a master's degree, write a book or receive a promotion, but there are things you do not yet know that will also lead toward your fulfillment. The people you will meet, the self-confidence that will emerge, and the self-improvement and knowledge that you will gain are going to give you unexpected opportunities and long-term fulfillment.

PERSONAL AND PROFESSIONAL SUPPORT SYSTEMS

Good support systems are essential in many ways as you strive to reach your larger life goals. Going back for your

MBA or writing a book is something you can't do alone. You can sit through all your MBA classes alone, but you need the help of people who believe in you and can encourage you to keep going when you want to give up. In addition, having personal or professional support systems that hold you accountable for reaching your life goals increases your chances of being successful in meeting those goals. If you don't have strong support systems or are not seeing a professional to help guide you toward fulfillment, be sure to hold yourself accountable by setting up reward systems.

There are several things to consider when putting together and tapping your support systems. First, in order to get those who are part of your support network to buy into your plans, you truly have to believe you can attain your goals. Don't get people involved in something you are not going to commit to or do not have the means to complete. The goal you set has to be attainable given your unique lifestyle and you must believe you can achieve the goal. It goes back to having confidence. Remember, while men might use aggression to achieve goals, SuperWomen use confidence. As women, our confidence is what empowers us to fight through barriers and negative self-beliefs.

You will also need supporters who accept that you need to take time for yourself while you push toward fulfillment. Working toward a life goal may mean that you have to spend less time for a while with those who are part of your top five life roles. You'll also be calling on those very people to help you.

So remember to treat your supports with respect. As I've talked about before, be willing to give them quality time and attention when it's time to focus on them. The more satisfied your support systems are with the attention you provide them, the less guilt you'll feel when you take time for personal fulfillment. Not only that, but if those who are part of your top life roles are satisfied, that gives you the green light to set more goals.

HANDLING FEEDBACK AND CRITICISM

When setting and working on your goals, you also want those in your support systems to be honest with you. It's better that your partner let you know when you are getting off track than having your boss or other people in the community tell you. Being able to accept constructive criticism can be hard at times, however. For all of your goals, be receptive and examine the feedback people give you on your performance. Don't take the feedback too personally or get outraged.

Keep in mind that there's a difference between someone who is helping you identify weaknesses and encouraging you to work through them and someone who is overly critical and hurtful. Take the opinions and feedback from the people within your top five life roles seriously. They are the most important people in your life. As for those outside that circle, you can acknowledge their feedback and then assess whether or not it's worth considering what they have to say.

If criticism from others has pained you in the past or created intense emotions, first identify who provided you with that criticism. Was it from someone you respected and whose opinion you valued? Or was the criticism from someone to whom you had handed the key to your life, allowing them to control your emotions? If criticism that hurt you in the past came from a valuable support, perhaps it's time to complete an honest reflection of yourself and see where you can improve. If the criticism came from someone in the other category and you have allowed that person to hinder your progress toward success and fulfillment, take back your key today.

Often we hold on to advice from people whose opinions we don't actually value because of the intense negative nature of their comments. We then begin to internalize the negativity instead of seeing the comments for what they are actually worth. People who are negative and go around holding back other people are often fighting their own personal battles. A SuperWoman knows it's best to allow negative people to fight their own battles. She doesn't internalize their criticism. She forgives them and then drives forward toward her own success.

How Not to Give Up

This chapter wouldn't be complete without talking about what to do when you're tempted to give up on your goals. Defining a life goal may be easy to moderately difficult, but the journey toward obtaining that goal is usually difficult. Don't let your barriers stop you. If you really want to feel fulfilled, be open to accepting that the journey is not going to be easy. But don't fear that the journey will be too difficult either. Fear of failure will lead you down a nonfulfilled life path or convince you to never start a goal in the first place.

People say it's easy to quit, but I think quitting is the hardest thing to do. The hard part about quitting is that it brings with it regret and long-term lack of fulfillment. When women think about quitting or do quit, they have guilt or anxiety about giving up. These feelings are painful. Some-times, regret for not finishing a life goal lasts days, weeks, months, years, or even a lifetime.

Realize from the start that obtaining a goal takes strength. You will need strength from your mind, your body, and your supports. Imagine the following scenario. You put your back up against a wall and hold one leg up in the air. Your goal is to hold your leg up in the air for 30 minutes. This goal is measureable and attainable. It's not an easy goal to obtain, but it can be done.

When you first put your leg up in the air, you may find that it's somewhat easy to do so. After a short time, it takes more of your body's systems to keep your leg up. Your stomach and back are now playing a role in this achievement. You begin to encounter barriers. Your leg is shaking and you're not even sure that this is the goal you wanted to work toward. You start to have self-doubt and lack confidence that you'll be able to keep your leg up in the air for the full amount of time. You realize that you need some support to help you keep your leg up. (I didn't say you had to hold your leg up all by yourself!) So you ask someone to hold your leg up for you.

You encountered barriers and found that it wasn't easy to hold your leg up in the air for 30 minutes, but instead of giving in you found a way around it and moved toward your goal. You learned that if you wanted to reach your goal badly enough, you could find a way to do it. You just had to use other resources and come up with solutions to the barriers. You'll most likely have to take the same approach with your life goals, opening up not only to support but also to creative solutions to stay in the game. Creative solutions are going to arise within the shades of grey. If you find yourself looking at only two options (this or that, black or white), step back and reassess. A SuperWoman knows that there is always more than a black-or-white solution to a problem. Remember, quitting is the hard part, so take the easy road and find an alternate route to your goal.

What else can you do when you want to give up on a goal? Try to reflect on why you set that goal in the first place. Passion and hope start you on just about any journey. When you are strong and in a positive place in life, open up your journal and list all the reasons you started toward your goal. That way, whenever your barriers get the best of you and you want to give up, you can turn to the list of why you wanted to obtain this goal and continue marching on toward fulfillment.

You can also pull out your old journals and reflect on them. Talk to friends and supporters and look at old photos as you ponder why you began this particular journey. Think about what you want for your long-term fulfillment. Remind yourself once again that your goals can be revised as you hit hurdles and bumps.

Anything that goes uphill takes more strength than staying stationary. Riding a bike up a hill is not easy. Holding your leg up in the air for 30 minutes is not easy. Even driving a car uphill requires more energy from the car. The engine has to work harder to pull you up that hill. If going up is tough in almost every situation, don't think that moving closer to your goals will be easy either. However, when you climb a mountain and you finally make it to the top, you get to look around and see what you accomplished. You look at the horizon, look at the base of the mountain where you took your first steps, look at everything between your feet and the start line. That's the journey *you* took. All of that led up to this moment of fulfillment.

When you reach each of your own goals, do the same thing. Breathe in the newfound confidence. Look at the barriers and fears you left behind. Look at where you're finally standing. The journey toward fulfillment isn't going to be easy, but it will be worth it.

~

If you don't know where you are going,
you'll end up someplace else.

—YOGI BERRA

My SMART Goals

List three goals you want to begin working toward or are currently in the processes of obtaining. Follow the SMART model to write them out as specifically and concisely as possible. Set some time aside for this exercise so you can develop well-honed goals that are specific, measurable, attainable, realistic, and time-bound.

Example:

GOAL 1:

S (specific): *I will lose 10 pounds.*

M (measureable): *I will track my weight loss by stepping on the scale once per week and by using the BMI machine at my local gym with my trainer.*

A (attainable): *I will work out three times per week and not eat after 7 p.m. I can do this.*

R (realistic): *I will not starve myself or limit my food so much that I can't handle this change. I can get to the gym three times per week based on my work schedule. This is realistic for me and my current lifestyle.*

T (time-bound): *I will lose 10 pounds in two months.*

GOAL 1:

S (specific): _____

M (measureable): _____

A (attainable): _____

R (realistic): _____

T (time-bound): _____

GOAL 2:

S (specific): _____

M (measureable): _____

A (attainable): _____

R (realistic): _____

T (time-bound): _____

GOAL 3:

S (specific): _____

M (measureable): _____

A (attainable): _____

R (realistic): _____

T (time-bound): _____

SuperWoman Skills

I create SMART goals to work toward fulfillment.

A SuperWoman makes sure the goals she sets are
specific, measureable, attainable, relevant, and *time-bound.*

A SuperWoman uses confidence to achieve goals.

A SuperWoman prioritizes and keeps in mind
her life roles when setting and working on her goals.

A SuperWoman knows that she does not need
to work on all her life goals at once.

A SuperWoman understands that personal or professional
support systems increase her chances of being successful.

A SuperWoman accepts constructive feedback
and does not internalize criticism from negative people.

A SuperWoman does not give up but finds
creative solutions to keep working toward her goals.

CHAPTER 6

TRACK YOUR WAY
TO SUCCESS

~

Not only is setting goals important but so is tracking your success each step of the way. Did you know that 90 percent of people who write down their goals reach their goals? For heaven's sake, put those goals on paper and the odds will be in your favor!

Over the years, there are probably many goals you've reached that you never wrote down. However, when you write down a goal, you'll find that you'll strive harder and more efficiently to achieve that goal quickly. Once you see that you have achieved a goal, you'll also get a boost of confidence that will propel you into immediately setting another goal. All of those behaviors bring you closer to self-actualization and super fulfillment.

Have you ever watched children play video games? When they see that they have won at a certain level and are advancing right away to the next level, they keep going. If the game didn't tell them that they had won, they might be inclined to stop playing or come back to it later. I want you to think in a similar way when it comes to setting your goals. When you see your progress and know that the gates are open to the subsequent level, you will walk right into that next step without even knowing it.

In this chapter, you're going to learn more about why it's important to track your successes along with some tips for doing it effectively. Initially, this process may seem tedious or meaningless, but there truly is a difference between having goals in your head and actually writing them out and observing your progress. When you visually see your progress, you will be consciously—and more importantly, unconsciously—motivated to keep moving toward your goals.

Stay Positive and Don't Compare

Before you begin tracking your progress, there are a couple of ground rules to keep in mind. First and most importantly, *think positively.* As you move toward your goals and fulfillment in life, there will be bumps, bruises, and barriers. Life is a journey and so is finding fulfillment. Bumps are a part of that journey. Sometimes they even make fun memories. The catch here is that you have to be positive in good times as well as tough times.

In addition, you really have to believe in this principle that thinking in a positive way will bring positivity and goodness to you. If you just say that but don't believe it, it won't work. This is similar to what happens to people who say they want to change but don't really want to change. They never end up changing. When you really believe good things are coming, you set yourself up to bring positivity into your life and you take action to make it happen.

Ground rule number two for success tracking is *do not compare yourself to others.* You are you. You are not him and you are not her. You can improve, change, and adapt, but you still won't be him or her. Have you ever met people who are trying to be someone else? They try to look or act like another person and that seems out of character for them. You might have been amused at how hard they were trying to be someone else because you knew that they would never become that other person. In fact, the time and energy they expend on comparing themselves to others reduces their chances of becoming self-actualized and fulfilled. We can observe this behavior in adolescents. They try to imitate a character from a favorite television show or try to act like the popular girl at school does.

At one time or another, we all tried to act like someone else but eventually found that that wasn't possible. You're not being fair to yourself by stepping onto someone else's life scale when you are measuring your own goals. That doesn't mean you cannot have role models and mentors. You can admire certain characteristics in others, such as their motivation or integrity. You can use a role model's life path as a guide to help you. You can mimic fashion styles. But the one thing you cannot do is become someone else. Their past is different, their biology is different, and there is a lot you don't know about them. You are in control of you, and you need to use your time and energy to explore who you are instead of rating yourself against someone else. In the final analysis, you might not even want to be like that person after all.

When we try to keep up with Mrs. Jones, we create guilt. We think, *How does she do it? What am I doing wrong? Will my children suffer? Is my husband happy?* Comparing yourself to others also sets you up for failure because you are rating yourself against something you don't fully understand or know. You have no idea about the realities of what Mrs. Jones is going through. You're just assuming what happens behind the scenes in her life. If you are rating yourself on a faulty scale, expect faulty results.

I tried to keep up with the Joneses at one time. Mrs. Jones puts her kids to bed at 7:30 p.m., if you didn't know that. My children are up well past that. I found myself becoming upset that the children were up until 10 p.m. What kind of mother was I? Actually, when I stopped comparing myself to Mrs. Jones, who I don't even personally know, I realized that I'm a great mother. My husband and I both work from home. I get to take my oldest son to school and pick him up every day. He is academically and behaviorally doing very well. Both my children are happy, rested, and healthy.

The reality is that what I'm doing works for my family and makes us successful as a family.

If you look at what someone else is doing and see a way to improve that's a good fit for you, that's fine. But criticizing yourself as you go about your daily life, as you set your goals, and as you measure your success in reaching those goals—simply because you do something differently than someone else—can be detrimental to your decision-making process, mental health, and overall fulfillment.

TRACKING PROGRESS WITH A SCALE AND JOURNALING

As you begin to track and rate your progress toward attaining your goals, think about your personality type and what kind of system will get you visually or mentally stimulated to continue moving forward. One way to track your progress is using what is called a Likert scale. A Likert scale is a way to rate the intensity of certain variables. For example, let's say your goal is to improve your overall mood. Each week, you would track your mood on a scale from 1 to 10, 1 being a depressed and negative mood and 10 being the best possible mood you could have.

As you track your weekly mood, I suggest you also journal so you can pinpoint why your mood was at a 5 during some weeks and an 8 during others. When you journal, you can more easily look back to see if it was hormones that played a role in your mood, interactions with certain people, lack of exercise, what you ate, or certain thoughts. Reflecting on your behaviors by reviewing your journal entries will give you more awareness and therefore more control in seeing where you need to change your thoughts or actions. This should lead to more frequent highs in regard to your mood on your Likert scale.

Journaling as you measure your progress in reaching goals is also helpful because our barriers are not always obvious to us. Sometimes you have to take a step back and visually see your thoughts or actions on paper in order to see your barriers. You might think, for instance, that you don't fear anything or that you aren't self-critical or pessimistic. However, when you write down your thoughts, experiences, and interactions and go back at a later date to reflect on them, you create an entirely different situation for your brain. Your brain has now had time to reflect on situations and events as an outsider. You are the third party reflecting on an event from the past and you may uncover patterns you didn't observe at first.

Going back to things at a later time also means you have a stronger and a clearer head to work with—a head with less emotion, less negativity, and more commonsense. Journaling and self-reflection helps you combat the tendency to act before you've thought things through. People who are impulsive tend to react, retreat, and then rethink. You want to *retreat, rethink, and then react.*

When you take time to reflect on an issue, you are also more aware of the reality of the situation versus what you assume to be true. In your journey toward self-fulfillment, you want to acknowledge your own flaws and avoid having biases. You might notice that you are strongly in favor of or against certain people or things. Perhaps you make unfair decisions or act certain ways when you come into contact with those people or things. That's a bias. When you reflect on your progress and your journal writings, be open and honest about what you observe. You may discover that you are very critical of others or that you are avoiding issues or lack boundaries.

FOCUS ON SELF-ACTUALIZATION NOT PERFECTION

We all have flaws, and that's okay. As you track your progress, accept that you are not perfect. Perfection is nonexistent. People who are perfectionists often don't find fulfillment even when they reach their goals. When perfectionists fail, they are very critical of themselves, leading to self-defeating beliefs and a reduction in confidence. This discourages them to reset new goals, further decreasing the potential for fulfillment.

Focus on becoming self-actualized rather than perfect. Self-actualization is the process of developing your full potential. A

SuperWoman knows that trying to be perfect or thinking she has to be perfect only sets her up for failure. If perfection does not exist and you are striving for something nonexistent, the odds are not in your favor. Besides, since life is subjective, what seems "perfect" to me would not necessarily seem "perfect" to you. That is why you don't want to spend your life trying to please other people. Your definition of being perfect will always be different from theirs.

In reality, those who are trying to seek perfection only stay at the same point in life. They strive to make themselves better and their lives better, but whatever they do is still not good enough for them. Perfectionists put themselves in a never-ending circle with no way out. They keep chasing improvement but never give themselves credit when they deserve it; they only see the need for more improvement.

A SuperWoman is well aware that she can always improve herself. However, when she reaches a goal or makes a life change she is proud of, instead of seeing how far she could still go, she celebrates her success. By celebrating your successes, you are bringing your accomplishments into your awareness. That, in turn, boosts self-confidence and life fulfillment.

TRACKING WITH THE THERMOMETER METHOD

In coaching sessions, I make use of a thermometer as an effective method for tracking progress. Here is how the thermometer tracker works. On a sheet of paper draw a thermometer without all the dashes. At the very top of the thermometer, write your ultimate goal. The goal must be dated, realistic, and achievable. For example, the top of the thermometer could read "Get into Graduate School for Business—September 2015."

Divide your thermometer into sections based on how many weeks there are between your goal start date and end date. Each week, in your journal or on a calendar, create smaller goals that you must achieve within that week. Week one's goals might be to "research top business schools" and "select a date to take the GMAT prep course." At the one-week mark, assuming you have reached your goals for that week, you would begin to color in the thermometer for that specific week.

You will slowly begin to see your progress as you color in each week and get closer to the goal line at the top. Be sure that each week when you reach your goals, you reward yourself, as a SuperWoman would do. Do not short yourself and miss a week of rewards. Giving rewards encourages the brain at both conscious and unconscious levels to create healthy habits.

The Danger of Living in Crisis Mode

So far in this chapter we've focused on highlighting and tracking our successes. It's also important to understand what can hinder, impede, or steer you away from success. The more you're aware of what not to do, the higher your chances of becoming successful. Next you'll explore two major habit patterns that can impede your ability to note, highlight, track, and achieve success: *making decisions in crisis mode* and *being negative.*

Have you ever met people whose lives seem to be awesome? Good things happen to them, one right after another. Their children are always doing well in school, their cars never break down, and they are promoted every year. If something does come up in their lives that constitutes a negative, it doesn't seem to crush them. In contrast, have you met people you almost always feel bad for? They just can't seem to catch a break in their lives. Their child is always sick, they're hitching rides to work because their car broke down again, and they never get the promotion they deserve. It's one negative thing after another. They live their lives in crisis mode every day.

Life is a bunch of ups and downs for everyone. If life and its journey were laid out, it would look something like this:

The difference between the people who always seem to "have it good" and those who "can't get a break" is that those who "have it good" make decisions at the high points in their lives. If you are in a depressed or angry state, are going through a divorce, are failing at something, or have recently lost a family member or your job, you are not ready to make a major life decision. When you are going through a major change or are at a low point in your life, there is probably a lot of emotion involved. When emotion becomes dominant in decision making, the decision is often not the right decision. It's a decision made out of spite, revenge, anger, sadness, or desperation and not out of clear mindedness, analysis, or basic commonsense.

Some of the most savvy business people are successful because they do not make decisions based on emotion. We might think these types of individuals are heartless. Perhaps they chose to fire a single mother who is late to work three times a week and is trying to juggle children, work, school, and a divorce all on her own. Her anxiety and depression are forcing her to live in crisis mode.

While I agree that letting this single mother go might seem mean, on the other hand it might be a good business decision. This woman may be costing the company a lot of money and her behaviors might rub off on other employees who think that if she can come in late, so can they. If I say to you, "I think this boss is mean for firing the single mother,"

I am coming from a place of emotion. I am upset or angered by what looks like the boss's insensitivity to this woman's life situation. Yet you can see that if the boss were to base decisions on emotion and on how everyone else feels, it's likely that the business would not be successful.

People who live in crisis mode are forced to make decisions from their emotions. That pattern of bad choices and decisions cycles their self-esteem down and their self-doubt up. When you make a decision out of strong emotion, you are more likely to make a subsequent choice in which emotion or impulsivity, not clarity and a well thought-out process, play a major role.

To see how this cycle works, let's look more closely at the mother who was let go from her job because of her consistent tardiness. She's juggling work, school, children, and a divorce—four areas of her life that are strongly rooted in emotion. Her survival and her children's depend on her job. School is her hope for her future. Her children are what she fights for. And a divorce is often filled with some of the strongest emotions we possess—anger, sadness, and pain. She is living in survival mode each day and feels that she must choose between paying extra money for early childcare or arriving to work late 15 minutes each day. She knows the late policy, but to save money she chooses to opt out of early childcare.

That choice has consequences. It means she has to race to work every morning so she won't be too late. That starts the day off on the wrong foot, in a stressful, rush-rush state. This behavior becomes a habit. She's always rushing and her life is full of choices between the lesser of two evils. When she's finally let go from her job, she's forced into another rush—making a decision about where to work and what to do for money. It's a new crisis full of emotion and anxiety. Her anger about being let go and her anxiety and sadness about what is happening will inevitably steer her into making an emotionally based decision.

The immediacy of everything in this woman's life and the emotions involved keep her from being able to see all the options available and from taking part in the retreat, rethink, react plan that would help her make the best decision. In this state, it wouldn't be surprising if she ended up in a new job she didn't enjoy from day one or in a job where she went on to make the same mistakes all over again. For example, because she feels desperate, she might take another job that starts at 8 a.m. and find herself once again racing to work each morning. This rush-rush continues to keep her life in crisis mode.

OPENING UP YOUR OPTIONS

Making one bad decision after another at the low points in our lives is the equivalent of never getting a break. On the other hand, those who come from a place of positive thinking and who make decisions at high points in their lives set themselves up for making a second positive decision and so on. The more clear-minded and positive your thought process is, the more options you'll realize are available to you. And the more you live in crisis mode, the more you'll narrow your vision. Why? Because when you're in a situation that seems overwhelming with too much going on, your mind shuts down options.

Your mind is doing its best to handle everything on your plate but may eliminate options in order to minimize how much you perceive you are taking on. That's when you start to see things only in black and white. When you see things as black or white (this choice or that), you minimize your potential for growth and happiness because you've limited yourself to only one choice or the other—that's it. But life is not black and white only. Life happens in the shades of grey and you always have other options.

You can turn around the habit of being in crisis mode and making decisions at low points by staying positive and taking time when making decisions. "Stay positive" is not just a cliché. When you engage in positive thinking and give your mind time to process a situation, you open yourself up to seeing the wider range of choices currently available to you.

We have a lot of resources available to us, but when we live in crisis mode, we often overlook them. We are used to doing things by ourselves or repeatedly telling ourselves: "I have to do everything on my own." The more you tell your mind something, the more your mind believes it. So if you are always saying that you don't have help and you go ahead and do everything by yourself, you'll come to believe that you have limited resources and you'll find that you are doing almost everything on your own.

When you're caught in this pattern, remember to take a moment to retreat, rethink, and then react. Take a step back and honestly reflect on your situation. When the emotion dies down, begin to look for the shades of grey in your life. Stepping back will help you reflect on the resources around you, such as friends or family, programs, communities, and networks. These are all places where we can go for help, but when we're blinded by emotion or pain we aren't able to see that we have these resources. Yet it's help from others that assists us through decision making and gets us through one crisis situation and not into another one.

What would the retreat, rethink, react plan look like for the mother in our example? Although she needs to get a new job immediately, instead of rushing into something that she'll dread and that will deplete her energy and keep her in crisis mode, it would be in her best interests to take one day to relax. You will be amazed at how much sorting out your mind can do in one day of rest and focus. By taking a day to sort out her thoughts or even walk around her community, she may find that she has more people to help her than she once thought. She may decide that contacting a university to go back to school part time might reignite some of her passion and help her in the long term. She might remember an employee she once worked with and reach out to her to see if her new place of employment is hiring. When you're in a situation like this, by taking a moment to step back and think outside the box about all your resources, you may find that you have many more options than you once thought.

The other very important plus about positive thinking is that if we have mostly positive days and positive thoughts, we store up so much energy that when we hit a bump in the road we can battle the barrier with limited force and still win. In contrast, when we live in crisis mode, we deplete our energy every day and have nothing stored up that we can use when a major crisis hits.

The brain, in a resting state, consumes approximately 20 percent of your body's energy. Thus, even in a clear-minded state of rest, you are expending energy. When you are in crisis mode, you can expect to expend at least double or triple the amount of energy as when you are not in crisis mode. Reflect on what kind of thoughts and actions use up your energy every day. I tell my clients to think about it like this. You get 20 energy dollars per day. *Use them wisely.* If you only had 20 dollars to spend each day, you would focus on what counts and matters most to you and your family. Would you spend 5 of your 20 dollars buying someone else's old shoes? No! So why would you want to spend your energy dollars on feeding into someone's gossip, holding grudges, complaining about your boss, or worrying about things that don't really matter. Take your energy dollars and spend them on what matters to you and your life.

Reframing Negative Situations

The million dollar question, of course, is how do you stay positive in a negative situation—and how do you begin to believe in the idea that "if I'm positive, positive things will come"? The trick is in reframing the situation. In every bad situation, there is a different or lighter way to view what happened. Even if you have to reframe something devastating as a learning lesson, that will help you move forward. If we sulk, we hinder our forward progress. If our progress is hindered, we stay in the same spot we're in—anger or sadness. That is not to say that when it comes to losing someone due to a death or divorce that we shouldn't grieve. Grieving is a natural and healthy process. We need to take the time to engage in the grieving process so our bodies can heal.

Here's how you might reframe a difficult situation at work. Some of us are unhappy in our careers. If you acknowledge that you have a choice to work where you are now, the situation immediately becomes lighter because you know that ultimately you do have an out. You are not bound by law to work there. It may not be easy to leave this particular job for various reasons, but the very fact of believing that you could leave gives you peace of mind. You know that you have options. They may not all be options you like, but at least you have some choices.

If you have decided that you are not going to leave your job, you must accept your decision. Do not make every day of your working life miserable by complaining about and regretting your circumstance. You have chosen to stay. Avoid brainwashing yourself by gossiping with co-workers about how horrible your workplace is. Not only does gossiping help to consistently reiterate to your brain that your job is unfulfilling, but it also means you are allowing yourself to associate with people who fuel your fire. That further validates in your mind that your workplace is negative. Additionally, bosses and managers observe this behavior. Being negative may lead to the loss of an advancement opportunity that may have put you in a position to enjoy your career.

If you work really hard in your career but feel you are not noticed, instead of blaming authorities, look at yourself and what you can control. If you continually say that your boss doesn't notice you, you are putting the control in his or her hands. That only leaves you feeling that you have no recourse and that you are pretty much at a standstill in your career. But when you acknowledge that you were passed by for promotion because of something *you* did or did not do, you are putting yourself in control of what's happening to you. You realize that you are the one who has the ability to change the situation and promote yourself.

What can you do? You can work hard, avoid gossip, and show that you are definitely qualified for a promotion. Speak up. Have you gone to the correct people and departments to show off your work? Have you marketed yourself to them? Sell yourself. If you sit back, someone else will snatch the opportunity. If someone else received a promotion instead of you, look at what characteristics they have that you may lack. What do they perform better at? Ask mangers what you can do to improve and how. Ask for more leadership roles. If someone unfairly received a promotion, maybe it's time to look in other areas of the company or outside the company for further opportunities. Maybe you have to go a longer route and go back to school or get extra training.

Choices are not always easy to make and sometimes our choices mean choosing between the lesser of two evils. Regardless of the situation you're in, you do have choices and you do have control. Reframe each situation and you'll begin to believe that your positive thinking does create a positive life. With each event and circumstance comes a choice of how to act or react. Psychiatrist, Holocaust survivor, and author Viktor Frankl said it best when he wrote that, even in the worst of circumstances, one has the freedom "to choose one's attitude."

You now have in hand many tools for success tracking that can help you stay focused on your goals and help you avoid the pitfalls that can trip you up along the way. Tracking your goals and successes is, in essence, a never-ending process. That's because you will continually be rating your progress on the different goals you work toward. When you meet one life goal, you will be aligning yourself with an opportunity to begin working toward another life goal. When it's time to start toward that new goal, you can come back to this chapter, remind yourself of the principles and tools you've learned, and begin tracking your progress toward success once again.

~

To tend, unfailingly, unflinchingly, towards
a goal is the secret of success.

—Anna Pavlova

Tracking My Progress

You may have already created your own tracking system, researched one you like, or want to try using a scale or thermometer with journaling to measure your progress. Choose a method that will work for you.

Now go back to the goals you set in chapter 5 and create a visual of how you will measure your goal. If you are using one of the methods I discussed in this chapter, reread the instructions above under "Tracking Progress with a Scale and Journaling" or "Tracking with the Thermometer Method."

Keep your visual (for example, your drawing of the thermometer divided into weekly segments) in a key place so it will motivate you as you watch your progress each day. When you wake up, you should be able to look at the direction you've set for your day, and when you go to bed you want to see your successes.

SUPERWOMAN SKILLS

I track my progress toward my goals.

A SuperWoman writes down her goals and
consistently tracks her successes.

A SuperWoman does not compare herself to others
as she sets goals and tracks her progress.

A SuperWoman rewards herself when she
meets small and large goals.

A SuperWoman strives for
self-actualization, not perfection.

A SuperWoman does not live in crisis mode.

A SuperWoman retreats, rethinks, and then reacts as her
primary method for decision making.

A SuperWoman reframes her negativity to
remind herself that she does have choices and control.

CHAPTER 7

REACH OUT FOR SUPPORT

~

We all need support systems on our journey toward fulfillment. No one is strong enough to get through life alone. Thinking you are strong enough to do it all by yourself can lead to anxiety, depression, and health-related problems.

Marilyn Monroe once said, "A woman can't be alone.... A man and a woman support and strengthen each other. She just can't do it by herself." I certainly don't think every woman needs a man, and if I could revise and update this quote, I would say: "A woman needs support systems. Support systems strengthen the already strong woman. No one can get through life alone. We all need support." It does take time to create support systems that are healthy, but it is worth it.

One thing I've learned from single mothers is that it's okay to ask for help. Many single mothers don't hesitate to reach out for an extra hand. The ability to ask for help and set aside feelings of guilt makes these women stronger, more efficient, and more productive. It truly does "take a village to raise a child." There is a reason that saying reads that way and not "It takes one person to raise a child."

The same is true for you and your life goals. Look at any goal you have and know that at some point you'll need support to achieve it. Don't be too prideful, fearful, or shy to ask for help. You're still a SuperWoman if you ask for help. In fact, the more help you take advantage of, the more super and super fulfilled you will become.

Though I said that single mothers are often good at seeking support, many women and mothers do struggle to ask for help when they need it. Society has a pretty effective way of making women feel guilty if they aren't chauffeuring 14 children to 10 different sports games, all while making a five-course dinner and having the children in bed before 9 p.m. That's what the Joneses do, right?

I talked about the danger of comparing ourselves to others. Who cares what the Joneses do! You don't know the circumstances of their life. Maybe they have an on-site nanny or the mother doesn't have to work and has plenty of time on her hands. Maybe they secretly hate sports altogether but are taking part in those programs because they think they need to prove something to someone. Or maybe they genuinely are happy transporting these children around town. Whatever the reason, they are not part of your top five life roles, so don't waste your time trying to figure out their lives.

Don't let society or other people manipulate you into thinking you should do things a certain way. Don't let your assumptions about other people's perceptions impact decisions you make for your family. SuperWomen march on in a direction that is good for them and their families. That means that if you've always wanted to attend an art class and a mature and supportive neighbor can watch the children while you go, ask your neighbor to lend a hand. You are still a good mother if you engage in activities aimed at helping or enjoying yourself. You are actually a *better* mother when you do things that help you stay in balance.

Don't Write Yourself a Prescription for Anxiety

You do not get an award for "doing it alone." The only thing you get when you overwhelm yourself and do things alone is an increase in anxiety. The more you put on your plate, the higher the likelihood that you will have a breakdown. Having a high level of anxiousness takes energy and time. Anxiety can literally become a life role. Women even worry about how much they worry! If you try to "do it all" and, even worse, "do it all" by yourself, you have just written yourself a prescription for anxiety. If seeking help and support will increase your fulfillment and make your life easier, do it.

Another factor that adds to our anxiety is one that I've touched on before: trying to be perfect. In chapter 3, where you explored barriers to your fulfillment, one of the barriers I asked you to look at was perfectionism. Perfection is subjective and, quite frankly, doesn't even exist. If you strive to be perfect, you actually put yourself in a position where you are stuck doing everything alone. Why? Because what you perceive as perfect is usually not what I perceive as perfect. Thus, if I help you, you'll most likely think that I'm not doing anything correctly and you'll never ask me to help again—or you won't invite me to help in the first place. In effect, a perfectionist thinks she has to do everything herself in order for it to turn out "perfectly."

That can lead not only to anxiety and depression but also to a lack of fulfillment. Think about the unfulfilled people you know. It's likely that many of them are unfulfilled because they have spent their energies trying to take on roles they didn't really want to take on, they have attempted to please people they didn't even care to please, or they are perfectionists. In their attempt to take on too much, make everything perfect, and do things alone, they isolated themselves. Nothing is perfect about that.

Help Can Be Hiding in Plain Sight

Sometimes it can be challenging to identify who is or should be a part of your support system. You might even be surprised to learn that potential helpers are hiding in plain sight. I've discussed the importance of enjoying your journey and being in the present moment. As you become more present in the moments of your life, you'll actually be able to recognize the presence of supports that you did not even know existed. You might discover people in your life who have been there all along, people you never thought of turning to for support.

One very helpful source of support we sometimes overlook are the teenagers in our family. If you have adolescents, use them! I know that you are probably thinking that adolescents are takers by nature, but trust me—you can use them to your benefit.

Adolescents have been compared to infants and toddlers; they have a lot of physical changes going on. Toddlers have begun to explore their independence and want to discover all the new things they can do alone—crawl, stand up, walk, even unlock the door that leads to the pool. Yikes. The toddler has limited fear because he or she has not really experienced the world yet. Adolescents, too, are changing and exploring their new freedom. They have changing hormones, are trying to fit in, and are "testing the door to the pool." They have not experienced the real world and the fears and responsibilities it can pose. Just as an infant has to take, take, take to grow, so do adolescents. However, the big difference between a toddler and a teenager is that teenagers can carry heavier weights, and that means they can bring in the groceries and take out the trash.

Use the fact that your adolescent needs something from you to your advantage. What do you want done? Have your adolescent help you and let them know up front that they will be rewarded for assisting you. I am not saying that you should pay your children for every chore they do; there are appropriate levels of expectations and rewards. When you need support that goes above and beyond what you expect your teenager to contribute to the household, that's the time to reward them for their extra help.

One issue some parents have is that they believe it's their lawful duty to give their adolescent money for recreation. I don't believe that's true. Nor should you feel guilty for having them help and support you. You have to feed and clothe your children and provide them with shelter, so it's entirely acceptable to ask them for help in return. When you feel that they are deserving of money for recreation, give it to them. The catch is, whenever you give a reward of any kind to your child or adolescent, tell them why you are giving them the gift. This will reinforce their behaviors and build confidence. Explaining why you are giving them a reward will also increase the bond between the two of you and land you more help from your child.

Life is about balance and that includes a 50-50 balance in relationships. That 50-50 balance goes for your relationship with your children too. If your adolescent takes out the trash, makes the bed, and starts the laundry without you asking, reward them with verbal praise. If they go above and beyond whatever help you typically need, reward them with money or something they feel is desirable, remembering to tell them why they are receiving the reward.

I talked about the importance of credibility and not taking back your word in the first couple chapters. The same thing applies to your interactions with your children. Children can learn how to manipulate and take advantage of you and your authority if you don't hold to what you say you're going to do. When you don't come through on commitments, children lose respect for you. Always keep your promises. Follow through not only on the punishments and consequences you have promised your children for certain behaviors, but on your promised rewards too. You undermine your own authority when you create a punishment or consequence and do not hold to it. Staying true to your word increases your child's level of trust in you and also fosters a stronger rapport between you.

While your child is using the reward you have given them to go out and have fun, instead of allowing yourself to give in to the temptation to take out the trash yourself or start the laundry in their absence, go to that art class you wanted to attend or simply relax or meditate. If you choose to do otherwise, that is your decision. But I suggest you make the most of the newfound time that comes from learning to work with the potentially supportive people in your life in a mutually beneficial manner.

Sometimes it's hard to avoid the feelings of guilt associated with asking a child for help. Maybe you worked all day and have not seen your child. The last thing you want to do is ask him to complete chores. Mothers can also carry around a lot of guilt when their children are struggling in school or have an absent father. I want you to realize, though, that giving children small tasks to do and then rewarding them also benefits them. It increases their confidence and understanding of real-world principles.

Having children help you with tasks also gets them up and moving as opposed to sitting, where anxiety or depression can brew. Working on household tasks with your child can build a stronger connection between you and help your child open up and talk. In addition, the less housework you have to do, the more activities you can engage in that are fulfilling. And the more personal fulfillment you have, the more likely it is that your responses, interactions, and attitudes toward your children will be positive and valuable.

Overcoming Barriers to Asking for Help

When you begin to consider who to ask for support, there are other barriers you may confront that you didn't realize were there. Sometimes women fear that if they ask for help, they will "owe" the other person something in return. The fear of saying no to a person after they have already helped us can stop us from asking for help in the first place. You might fear that if a friend or neighbor agrees to help you out now, they will ask you for something later down the road that you might not be able or willing to give. Yet you don't even know if they will ask you for help; you're just assuming that. In fact, you don't even know if they will help you out to begin with. So you are allowing yourself to suffer without help because there's a chance they might need your help some day.

Don't let that fear stop you from seeking support. If this supporter does call on you for assistance in the future, you might find that the give and take of them helping you and vice versa proves to be beneficial in ways that you can't see now. On the other hand, don't feel that you always have to help someone who has helped you in the past. Your response to any request for help will depend on the situation you are in at that time.

In the event that you can help and want to help this person, be sure to do so in a way that doesn't turn you into a doormat. Set boundaries. If need be, you can say yes to some part of their request and no to other parts. If a friend wants you to pick up their child from school on Tuesday and you will be at the doctor, give them an option that better suits you but still shows that you want to help. A SuperWoman does things for other people but in a way that is convenient for her. This might sound like a selfish concept, but the more you can set boundaries in your life, the more positive you will feel. The better you feel, the more you will be able to give back. Always go back to the basic principle you learned at the beginning of this book: you have to give your time and attention to your top five roles before taking on anything else.

Toxic Friends and Partners

There are, of course, people I would not recommend reaching out to for help, such as those you know will sabotage you, those who love to find something "wrong" with you so they can hold it over your head, or those who belittle you or are manipulators. The benefit of asking those kinds of people for help does not outweigh the consequences. If you think you will experience more negativity and pain by asking them for help, in the long run it's not worth it. It will cost you too much energy, energy you could instead be spending on the important people in your life.

SuperWomen take time to assess the people in their lives and rid themselves of those who are toxic. The toxic people are those who suck you emotionally dry, stir up anger within you, or treat you like a doormat. Sometimes toxic people are fun and exciting, but the fun and exciting ones can possess the most toxicity, like the ex-boyfriend, the bad boy, or the female "best friend" who drags you down. The toxic girl-friend has time to gossip to you and about you. You talk to her over the phone, and when you hang up, you feel worse than you did when you initially called her. Get rid of her. It does not matter that you have known her since kindergarten. She is depleting your hard-earned energy dollars.

Likewise, it might seem easy to call on your old boyfriend to help you when your car breaks down. However, if having him help you makes you feel belittled or abused or you find that you give up your control and confidence when you're with him, remain without a car until you can come up with another solution. There is always another solution. If you can't think of one, you aren't taking enough time to analyze and reframe the situation.

You read about the dangers of black-and-white thinking in the last chapter. Black-and-white thinking—where the answer is this or that with no in-between—limits your brain being able to process and see other options. Without options, your control and positive life outlook decrease. Don't resort to black-and-white thinking. As a SuperWoman, you want to see what is in between the black and white. It may not be exactly what you want, but there is always another way to look at the same situation and come to a conclusion.

I advise women who are hooked on toxic partners to create a fantasy breaker—a list of the reasons you broke up with this person and why you don't want them back in your life. A toxic partner will not be different this time around. You broke up for a reason. Do not decide to go back with someone who hurt you and do not let your commonsense be outsmarted. That means you can't give in to the hooks they will try to use to get you back. Manipulative people are good at knowing what you love and then feeding you that in order to hook you or regain control. The more in control you now seem to be, the more a manipulator will try to give you everything you ever wanted. Bite the hook, though, and you're caught.

Who are the toxic people in your life? Toxic people can be the bipolars (the people who take you up and down with "I love you, I hate you"), the criers, the takers, the downright mean people, the users, the bullshitters, the gossipers, or the passive-aggressives (who get their digs in very subtly).

I understand that there are people who are toxic that you cannot or may not want to remove from your life. Mothers, fathers, or siblings can sometimes be toxic and very hurtful. If they must stay in your life, be sure to set clear boundaries with them. You can set boundaries with a family member or friend by saying no to them if you can't do something that they want you to do. You could also not answer their phone calls if you are busy or know that they are about to stir up drama. You must put the control back into your court. This means focusing on your life roles first and prioritizing what is best for you before doing something for them.

As hard as it is to accept responsibility for what happens in our lives, a SuperWoman knows that if she plans to keep toxic people in her life and then one of them hurts her, she is the one who ultimately let them in. It's your choice. You know their patterns and you labeled them as toxic, yet you kept them around and were willing to spend your energy dollars on them.

WHAT GOOD SUPPORTERS LOOK LIKE

How do you know who are the right people to reach out to for support? And what would a good supporter look like? First, realize that supportive people may not do everything in a way you consider perfect, but they genuinely want to help you. They are willing to take responsibilities off your plate, which will free you from stressors, give you more energy, and help you work toward fulfillment. Another quality of good supporters is that they bring to your awareness your negative behaviors.

That may seem counterintuitive, but here's why it's important. We don't always see when we are sabotaging ourselves. We can all be blinded by our own perceptions. We can be blinded by our perceptions of what we think is moral or right or by our perceptions of what is happening in a troublesome situation. For instance, a good support might bring to your attention your negative self-talk. Negative self-talk can decrease our confidence, increase our anxieties, and lead to depressive symptoms. We often do not hear the way we talk to ourselves. We need a good support to help us become more aware of how we treat our mind and body so that we can begin to work on those issues.

Think of a good support as a valued outsider who may have a different perspective on your behavior and on situations happening in your life. You might not always agree with that third party, but you should at least take what they have to say into consideration.

The reason honest feedback is beneficial is that if you aren't aware, for example, that you are controlling or that you engage in negative types of behaviors, how can you ever work through those barriers? If you are unable to identify your barriers, you won't be able to attain many of your life goals, and that will impact your level of life fulfillment. You must be self-aware to be self-fulfilled.

What are some issues that supports have brought up to you that you blew off at one time but that might constitute a barrier to your success and fulfillment? Don't let your ego or the need to be right stop you from answering that question. Be authentic with yourself.

～

Funny thing how when you reach out, people tend to reach right back. Best, then, to make sure your hand is open and not fisted.

—Richelle E. Goodrich

IDENTIFYING MY SUPPORT SYSTEMS

The exercise for this chapter is a two-part activity. The first part will help you will identify and reflect on the people who are part of your support systems. The second part will help you identify and deal with the toxic people in your life.

Start by creating a list of people you would consider to be a support to you. Make your list based on past experiences you have had with these people. Include both personal and professional supports. Under each person's name, write down the role that person plays in your life. Then reflect on and write down why you feel these people are supportive of you.

Keep this list in your journal and when you need help making decisions, are feeling blue, or need any other type of support, reflect on your list of supports and reach out to one of them. Feel free to list more than five names of supporters.

Example (Personal):

Name: *Wes*

Role: *Husband*

Why I consider this person to be a support: *When I am stressed out, he will take care of the kids and give me some space. He encourages me not to give up when I feel like quitting. He takes away my stressors by picking up extra tasks to relieve me from having to do them.*

Example (Professional):

Name: *Cindy*

Role: *Mentor*

Why I consider this person to be a support: *Provides me with direction for major business decisions. Is still confident in me even if I make a decision that did not give me the desired result. Educates me on areas where I have limited experience or need to grow. Helps me decrease my self-doubt in decision making.*

My Supports:

Now think about your own life and start creating your list of supports here:

1. Name:

    Role:

    Why I consider this person to be a support:

2. Name:

    Role:

    Why I consider this person to be a support:

3. Name:

   Role:

   Why I consider this person to be a support:

DEALING WITH THE
TOXIC PEOPLE IN MY LIFE

For this activity, pull out your journal or a notebook or use the space below to make a list of all the people in your life who are toxic—people who belittle or sabotage, who are emotionally or physically exhausting or abusive, or who bring pain into your life.

Toxic people in my life:

1. _____

2. _____

3. _____

4. _____

5. _____

Circle the names of those you know you can eliminate from your life first. Then erase them from your life just as you would hit the delete button on your keyboard. Don't call them on the phone and be sure to resist the urge to reach out to them for help.

Taking a step back from these people isn't always easy. I don't suggest directly telling these people that you will be taking a step back from them. That only opens the door to a discussion about why you are making this choice and you'll find yourself expending energy defending your point. You might also find that the manipulators have a way of sucking you back in to the point where you end up not getting rid of them. Instead of letting that happen, you have two options: immediately stop interacting with them or begin slowly backing off of any communication until there no longer is any.

Draw Boundaries:

Once you've committed to that first step for saying goodbye to the most toxic people in your life, think about the remaining ones on your list. Ask yourself:

- What attachment do I have to them?

- Why don't I want to get rid of them or why has it been hard to do so?

- Is there a way I can set boundaries with these people or wean myself from them?

Create a Fantasy Breaker:

If you find yourself hooked on a toxic partner or friend, create a fantasy breaker. List all the things you do not like about this toxic person and look at the list every time you have doubts about pulling away from him or her. Break the fantasy that your mind creates to trick you into taking this person back. False fantasies are barriers in disguise. Copy your fantasy breaker list to your phone and read it at least once a day.

As you work on eliminating the toxic people from your life and their influence fades away, you will find that have more time for yourself, your top five life roles, and your fulfillment.

SuperWoman Skills

I welcome and ask for support.

A SuperWoman takes time to assess
the people in her life.

A SuperWoman develops healthy support systems.

A SuperWoman stays away from negative people.

A SuperWoman rids herself of toxic people or
sets appropriate boundaries with them.

A SuperWoman accepts honest feedback about
her behavior and attitude from her valued supports.

CHAPTER 8

REFRAME YOUR STORY
TO SHOW YOUR STRENGTHS

~

Behind every woman, there is an amazing story of a journey that shaped who she is today. Whether that journey was made up of welcome changes or tough choices, women tend to minimize the high points of their stories. Some even fail to acknowledge them at all. When we minimize our story and the strengths and self-discovery our journey has brought us, we fail to give ourselves credit for why we are successful in life and in love. That works against the fundamental factor that upholds our confidence—the consistent reminder that we had and continue to have a worthwhile life journey.

Even if parts of your journey were difficult or painful, they can still have a positive impact on your confidence today. The trick is to learn how to reframe your past to work for you in the present—to know which version of your life story to tell and to tell it in a way that shows strength and resilience rather than portraying you as a victim to be pitied. The story you tell and retell about yourself shapes you in the present. So you want to be sure you are telling a story about your life journey that shapes the current you in the right way.

First, it's important to be aware that your journey is not something that simply happened in the past. It is ongoing. Every single day you should acknowledge that you are on a journey. The more aware you are that you are living your journey now and the more you tell yourself and the world about it in an appropriate and healthy manner, the more empowered you will feel.

Some of us have branched off and started new paths, but in the big picture, no matter how many paths we have taken, we are still on one big journey. If you look back at all the paths you have taken that make up your journey and you do not see any successes, you are looking at everything the wrong way. Instead, you need to reframe the situations you have experienced into something that is more beneficial to the person you are and who you are trying to become. That's the story you want to convey to others.

We tend to "tell" our stories in informal ways. Life isn't very formal. Most of the time, we aren't waiting to tell our stories at the right moment or at the right place. We unfold the story of who we are and where we have come from in every situation we encounter and in every conversation where we share something about ourselves. We tell bits and pieces to co-workers during work, to friends over the phone on the weekends, and silently to ourselves as we are cleaning the house, driving in the car, or showering.

The story that takes shape as we spit out bits and pieces of how we feel about our experiences becomes our perception of reality. Our perception of our reality then shapes our environment, emotions, and actions. In other words, as we tell and retell our story, we eventually become exactly what that story, in both its positive and negative aspects, says about us. In this chapter, you'll have the opportunity to look at how you've repeatedly told your personal story, how that has impacted who you are today, and how you can reframe your story to emphasize your strengths.

YOUR SUCCESSES AREN'T LUCK

One of the most valuable tips I have ever read came from Mika Brzezinski's book *Knowing Your Value: Women, Money, and Getting What You're Worth,* where she talked about women and the idea of luck. Women often have a faulty assumption that when something good happens to them it's because they are lucky. If we say we are lucky to have received a new job offer or are lucky to have been married for 40 years, we have created the potential for fear because we know that luck can run out. If, on the other hand, we worked hard for something, we know we earned it and it's not going anywhere.

So be honest. Didn't you work hard to qualify for that job offer or make your marriage last? Of course you did. When you get promoted or celebrate 40 years of marriage (or any other landmark anniversary or achievement in your life), acknowledge that you created that success over years of hard work, not through one quick draw of luck. If you take time to review your story and your journey, you will see that there were times when you may have had setbacks or even failures, but you were still successful in the end—you made it through and you gained something valuable in the process.

Your story conveys a message to the world and you are in charge of how you tell that story. If you want to look at yourself differently or you want others to see you differently, change some of the wording in your story. Many of us have had extremely hard or upsetting pasts, but we can reframe our stories to show our strength, resilience, and self-control in the face of those hardships.

When you think about your story in a manner that reflects strength and resilience, and you tell *that* story, believe in it, and live it, your confidence will continue to grow. Not only that, as you acknowledge and apply the lessons you learn from past experiences to your current and future experiences, you are shaping your present in a positive way and coming closer to self-actualization and fulfillment. As we highlight the successes and learning experiences in our stories that led to where we are now, we also become less fearful of loss, which can be one of the barriers to our fulfillment.

I admit that sometimes I forget to focus on the high points of my story, especially when I get scared that I am going to lose something. I have to remind myself that the more I tell my story of strength (or lack thereof), the more I become that version of myself. When my world gets rocky, I self-reflect and acknowledge that I need to begin focusing more on my story of strength, not on a story of pity. Sometimes I catch myself feeling that I am lucky to have had an opportunity or lucky to have my family. Then I realize that I shouldn't feel guilty saying that I positioned myself appropriately and worked my ass off for the opportunities that have come to me.

I have lots of stories that created who I am today. I have childhood stories, college stories, and motherhood stories. I could write 20 more chapters with all my stories. I could tell you stories that would make you cry and wonder why I never gave up. Those are pity-party stories though. Knowing that every experience of my past, whether bad or good, has contributed in a valuable way to making me who I am today, why should I tell my story in a depressing manner? I want to tell my story in a light that reflects my strength and my ability to overcome and achieve. I want to tell my story as the journey of success that it is.

I remember writing my dissertation for my doctoral program. I would work all day, then come home as my husband was leaving for work. Being a newlywed and a new mother, this was very tough emotionally and physically for me and my husband. When my husband would leave for work, he would pass me our newborn and all the responsibilities that came with him. I would sit with a pillow over my lap and nurse my son as I typed away at the theoretical foundation of my dissertation.

My husband and I did not live close to family and sometimes I felt really lonely. When my son was two and a half, we decided to move three hours south to be closer to our family. Then I got pregnant again and my husband lost his job. My thoughts at that time were "when it rains it pours," "Murphy's Law strikes again," "how unlucky can I get," and every other karmic line I could spout off. I found myself with a new full-time job and two new part-time jobs—one getting hours for licensure to become a mental health counselor and one as a professor. Meanwhile I was enjoying both the second and third trimesters of my pregnancy and my dissertation.

Hello! I worked my ass off for my success! Who am I kidding? Why should I let doubt minimize all I have done? I'm not lucky. Lucky people aren't being milked like a cow while trying to finish a doctoral program and working three jobs. So when I recall or talk about my days of being milked,

I try to focus on how that journey made me successful and helped me develop great life skills such as flexibility, openness to new experiences, and the ability to take feedback from mentors and supports. No, I'm not lucky, and that is a good thing. If my life was based solely on luck, I wouldn't be able to control my present or my future.

Let Go of Grudges and Move On

What is your story? You have one, even if you have great parents whose last name was Jones and you have never been milked like a cow. You have a story and a journey. Some women have stories that are hard to fathom, stories of overcoming childhood abuse, cancer, or surviving years of domestic violence. As tough as those stories are, they show the strength of the woman and what she has overcome.

It is challenging to accept our past sometimes, especially the simple yet painful truth that we cannot change it. If you had a traumatic or negative childhood, just remember that you are in control of your second family, where you become wife and mother or create your own community of close friends. A SuperWoman knows that she cannot control her first family, but she sure is in control of creating her second one.

Let go of grudges; they hurt only you. You are the one who has to live with those negative thoughts every day, no one else. Forgive the past and everyone in it so you can move forward. The best thing about forgiveness is that it is an action. You do not have to feel forgiveness—you just do it. You deserve freedom.

Regret is painful, especially when we take responsibility and ownership of a situation that we now regret. Our childhood or other situations that led to our holding grudges and regret are all unchangeable. What we *can* change is our perception of the negativity about the events. I am in no way saying that you must forget these experiences. Remembering them is important to your personal story. Rather, reframe the events into learning experiences that have made you strong enough to help, encourage, or protect others. Take your past and reframe it.

When you are fully aware and accepting of the fact that you can't change your past, you are more capable of doing something good with your story and your life in order to move forward. That is because you are not spending all your time and energy trying to prove how bad the past was. People who can't accept what can't be changed spend so much time dwelling on the situation that they do not have any energy left over to see how much power they do in fact have to reshape their journeys.

If you genuinely accepted your past and never dwelt on it again, how would you be different? How would you make different choices? How would your emotional state be different? If you have a negative story, how has your story of negativity hurt you or others in the past? Remember this: if *you* drink the poison of anger, don't expect the bad guy to die.

How to Highlight
the Positives in Your Story

As you look at the story you usually tell about yourself to see how you can reframe it to highlight what you have gained from your experiences, here are a few pointers. Talk about your journey so that you and others can see your strength and ability to adapt, change, and grow. Don't bore people with your endless problems and "I can't get a break" stories. Every woman is unique and has her own story separate from another's and there is no need to add in drama or beef up your story. So avoid telling your story in a manner that shows competition or comparison—"My story has more drama or intensity than yours."

Here's an example of a challenging life story that is told in a way that is not empowering or helpful: "I am always upset because when I was growing up my father was never around. He pawned off all the responsibility to my mother and then my mother pawned off half of the responsibility to me. And you know what? It doesn't change. I'm still the one who has to hold up everyone else. Typical that they always pawn off their problems to me. And when I need help, do you think they are there? Nope!"

Now imagine editing and retelling that story in the following way so that it highlights your strengths and learning experiences. "Growing up, I had a lot of responsibility. Although at times it was really tough for me to manage, you ought to see how good I am with follow-through and time management in my adult life. Having strong time-management and follow-through skills have landed me a management position at work and the ability to balance work, leisure, and family time without problems." As you edit your own story in a similarly empowering way, you will find a sense of fulfillment because you are affirming, not only to others but to yourself, that you are stronger than you may have given yourself credit for and have more successes in your past than you once thought.

Dwelling on the negatives in our stories as opposed to the positives creates more than one challenge along our path to fulfillment and meeting our goals. Your story is a representation of who you are today and a blueprint of who you are going to become. When you tell your story, you are creating your reputation—and you are exposing yourself to others who might not be kind as *they* retell your story. Not only can telling your story in disempowering ways lead to inappropriate gossip from others, but it can ruin your credibility, especially if you are a business owner. Mental health illnesses are still taboo to some people in society. In addition, people might associate your negativity with the type of service they would get if they used your business resources. They may also steer clear of you if they think they would have to provide you with too much support in a role as your partner or friend.

The other challenge we can create with sob stories about ourselves is that positive people will not be attracted to us. If you find yourself in a negative place, you need positive people in your life to you help change your path and create your new story. But guess what? You know why positive people are positive people? They stay far away from negative people. Negativity truly is contagious. The positive people you need in your life are going to politely decline the invitation to your pity party. So in order to get access to positive people, you will need to reframe your story and work day in and day out to convey a new message of strength and resiliency. Once you do that, you will begin attracting people who can help you steer your path in a positive direction.

HELPING OTHERS RESHAPE THEIR STORIES

If you have a story of strength and it has positively shaped your life, you can continue to grow by helping someone else reframe their story. Women have such inspiring stories of strength, and we must spread the word about those forms of success. We need to empower and encourage other women. I have noticed, unfortunately, that women can be really catty and hurtful toward other women. I see this quite a bit in business environments. Some women who get to the top don't push for other women to join them. Perhaps that's because of an unconscious fear of loss, a fear that they might lose their status by helping bring another woman to the top. Some women even choose to push others down. That's sad, but it is a reality. These women seem to be in competition with others when we should all be rooting for each other. I love this saying that I once came across: "Girls compete with each other; women empower each other."

It's important to understand that when you make it to the top or are enjoying your life, you have a unique opportunity to make life a little easier, a little brighter, or a little more successful for others, whether they know it or not. You can help change their story to be more positive—and in the process, you'll be changed for the better too. Instead of doing nothing or even subtly working to put down other women, be a SuperWoman and help edit their stories in a good way. Help them see how their stories can be reshaped. Educate them on the importance of reframing their past by focusing on how their experiences have made them stronger.

Often, we don't see our own strengths. Simply bringing to someone's attention that they are strong and resilient based on their past experiences could be the factor that bolsters their confidence and convinces them that they are capable of making important changes in their life. When we get stuck in the same negative life story, everything that comes our way seems like an obstacle. If you can show other women how many of those obstacles can really be seen as opportunities, you are helping them frame their life story in a more positive light.

Can you identify one woman who would benefit from your help? Would you be willing to help her reframe her story? Why or why not? If you are willing to help her, what is something you can do in the near future to give her a boost?

∾

Power consists to a large extent
in deciding what stories will be told.

—CAROLYN HEILBRUN

REFRAMING MY LIFE STORY
TO SHOW STRENGTH AND RESILIENCE

This activity will assist you in reframing your personal life story. First, take out your notebook and write your story as you would normally tell it—the story of how your life has un-folded, of who you are, and how you got to be where you are.

Walk away from the story and come back to it at a later date when you are feeling positive and happy. Read the story you wrote and ask yourself these questions:

• How would a positive person view this story?

• Would that person want to be around me?

• How can my journey be turned into a story of powerful-ness, strength, and resilience?

• What can I delete from or add to my story?

• What strengths or points of self-discovery didn't I men-tion?

Next, keeping your answers to those questions in mind, rewrite your story. Be authentic in telling your story, but reframe the negativity. You can acknowledge the challeng-es you faced, but dwelling on them in a negative way and creating an entire story based on how bad things were is not appropriate or effective. The more you tell your story in a negative manner, the more you personally reinforce the negativity in your life. Conversely, the more you tell your story in a positive manner, the more you personally reinforce the positivity in your life. Create a habit of telling a story of strength and you will become even stronger.

SUPERWOMAN SKILLS

**I reframe my life story to work for me
in positive ways in the present.**

A SuperWoman has identified and
embraces her true story.

A SuperWoman tells her story in a manner
that reflects strength and resilience.

A SuperWoman lets go of grudges, knowing that
they only hurt her and hold her back.

A SuperWoman knows that she isn't lucky
and that she has earned what she has.

A SuperWoman doesn't ask people to
bring balloons to her pity party.

A SuperWoman uses what she has learned from her own
challenging experiences to support and teach others.

CHAPTER 9

LIVING YOUR
SUPERWOMAN LIFESTYLE

~

SuperWoman, your time has come. Prepare your cape for takeoff. In the last eight chapters, you've learned a lot about yourself and you have already begun to develop empowering new skills and habits. You are ready to become a real SuperWoman—to achieve work-life balance and super fulfillment. You have finally decided to give up the juggling act you do so well, to take off all the different hats you've been wearing, and to put on one single cape.

Let's recap some of the key concepts you've started putting into action and that you'll keep in mind as you move forward. First, you have chosen your top five life roles (making sure the top one is you) and you have reflected on the importance of focusing on those roles and setting boundaries. You're no longer guilty about putting your own name on your priority list or taking time to find personal fulfillment.

As a budding SuperWoman, you know the importance of setting aside time for your own health and personal wellness.

You are cultivating the habit of being comfortable doing things you enjoy. You now see that staying forever busy and uncomfortable just to avoid feeling guilty when you aren't doing something for others is unhealthy and unnecessary. You realize that there are times when you have to ride the Ferris wheel and take care of your duties, but that's not all day every day. You know when to step off the revolving wheel and enjoy the moments of your life.

In addition, you have identified the specific barriers to your fulfillment. You have seen how barriers can decrease productivity, encourage less authenticity, make us feel guilty, or riddle us with anger. So you've taken the time to create a plan to overcome and stop being bullied by those barriers. You have also learned to create smart goals and use your confidence to achieve them as well as track your progress and reach out for support when you need it. Just as importantly, you have learned to reframe your life story to show how past challenges have gifted you with specific strengths.

As you continue to strengthen yourself with your new SuperWoman skills and lifestyle, you will create more energy to tackle other, less important "have to dos" in life. You may have already found that putting your new habits in place have helped you bank some extra energy dollars to rebound easily from setbacks. You know that a real SuperWoman does not choose to live in crisis mode. She doesn't rush decisions, takes time to look for other options, and gets help. She saves her energy dollars for major decisions and critical issues that could arise. When major issues do arise, she does not make decisions based solely on emotion and is not impulsive. She knows that making decisions at low points invites feelings of regret and guilt and that making confident decisions when she is positive and strong provides her with the potential for new opportunities and further fulfillment.

You Are in Control

You have the freedom to control your present, your future, and your fulfillment. Throughout this book, you've seen that taking control and responsibility are key traits of a Super-Woman. As a SuperWoman, you are willing to admit your faults and take responsibility for what is happening around you. As tough as it may be, you also take responsibility for your emotions and how you look at your life. You know that everything that happens is based on your perception of your personal reality—and that a change in perception will lead to change in your reality.

You have seen that life is subjective for all of us. What work-life balance means for me is different from what work-life balance means for you. The way I feel I should be treated in a relationship is different from the way you feel you should be treated. What I define as success might not be your definition of success. That is why you no longer strive to compare yourself to others when setting goals, caring for your family, or enjoying your life.

In your journey through this book, you've learned that pain, lack of fulfillment, and anxiety are based on our perception of the world and the interactions we have. You now know that if you have the power to create your own pain, you also have the superpowers to create your own happiness. Life is completely unfair at times. That's a true statement. There are no buts or whys; that's just how it is. A Super-Woman accepts that life can be unfair. But when she isn't holding the best cards in her hand, she *still* wins the round because her positive attitude trumps everyone. A positive attitude wins every time because it keeps us open to finding alternate solutions to winning and success.

What's Your Personality Type?

Most of us have been taught to think of ourselves as either a Type A or Type B personality type. How do you see yourself? Those with a Type A personality are proactive and overly organized. They are super achievers who take on way too much. They hate being late and don't like people around them being late. Those with a Type B personality want to achieve their goals but are not extremely upset when they do not. They are steady in their work and laid back about many things. Someone with a Type B personality can enjoy the moment.

I admit that if I had to choose, I would say that I am Type A. Although it is great to be successful and achieve (which both Type As and Bs do), the stress and torment that comes from the pressure I put on myself, sometimes unnecessarily, can affect my physical and mental health. Studies show that those with Type A personalities have double the chance of having a heart attack compared to Type Bs. When I learned about this, I thought "We're going to obtain all this success and achieve our dreams, only to then kick the can? That can't be good." The following saying reflects what can happen to a Type A personality: "A man spends his life getting his wealth, and then spends all his wealth on getting back his health."

Some people with Type A personalities live life at a stress level of 7 to 9 out of 10 day in and day out, whereas Type Bs have much lower stress levels. Living at a stress level of 9 is like living your life in crisis mode. We discussed that living in crisis mode is a real danger to your body emotionally and physically and that it also impacts your decision making. If you live in a fight-or-flight mode all the time and a real problem comes your way, you will find that you have depleted all your energy and aren't able to deal with the problem.

Think about it this way: If you were going to run a 5K race and before the race you ran for eight hours straight, you would already be out of breath when the time came to run the 5K. Why the heck did you run for eight hours straight before the race even began? That wasn't necessary. Similarly, if you run yourself to the ground trying to overachieve and perfectly perform every little activity in life, when you really need your energy you won't be able to perform.

It's habit patterns like these that cause mental breakdowns, panic attacks, and even attempted suicides. The body gets to a point where it cannot face expending another ounce of energy, let alone gearing up for a real battle. The body protects itself and sometimes it thinks that the best protection is to shut down. The problem is, your husband, children, job, and everything else on your list of duties still need you. You can't be down.

LIVING A TYPE S LIFESTYLE

Whether you've considered yourself as Type A or Type B, I'd like to introduce you to another option, one that I believe is a healthier way to look at yourself than either of those labels. It's what I call *Type S,* or *Type SuperWoman.* A Type S woman is strong. She's focused as well as balanced. Type S is workaholic meets Fijian islands.

Imagine you've just been transported with your work laptop on a raft near the shore of Fiji. Carlos the Cabana Boy is bringing you red drinks with little umbrellas and the wind is whisking your raft slowly down the shore. You have to stop and take in the moment. You are forced to. You do a little work, you kick a little sand, and then you go through that process again—until the drinks set in, at which time you get some much-needed rest. While few of us can relocate to Fiji, I do believe that we can find this balance of a little work, a little sand.

Welcome to the island of Type S personality. Type S seems like it should be easy to achieve (who doesn't like Carlos the Cabana Boy?). Actually, achieving a strong Type S personality is harder than one might think, especially because we are creatures of habit and easily succumb to guilt. People are who they are. It is quite challenging to change. If you have brushed and then flossed your teeth in that order for 40 years, it would be hard to suddenly change that order to floss then brush. Even if you did change the order in which you did this, after a couple weeks you would probably revert back to your old habit.

As you begin to work toward developing your Type S personality, you will discover that it is easy to let the trials of life or the quick pace of your lifestyle shove you once again into that Type A or Type B way of living, putting you right back on to the revolving Ferris wheel. Be patient and remind yourself of what you have learned here. Changing and self-improving takes time, and it can be a full-time life role. You must be present with yourself and aware of your choices, decisions, and actions every minute of the day. That takes work, but it's worthwhile work.

Don't judge yourself when you temporarily fall back into your old lifestyle. When you face challenges, as we all do, take a minute to open up your journal and review some of your past successes. Reflect on how far you have come. Note negative patterns of behavior you no longer engage in. You were able to propel yourself forward before, you were successful before, you knocked down barriers before. You will do it again.

Create Your Personal Vision Book

To help you keep on track and stay focused on your vision for work-life balance and fulfillment, I recommend that you take the time to create a vision book. During the Super-Women workshops, the women who are attending transform an empty scrapbook that I provide them into a vision book. You may have heard of the concept of a vision board. A vision book is similar to a vision board except that a vision book is made up of multiple pages. Each page is dedicated to one of eight different sectors of your life: physical health, emotional health, spirituality, professional life, marriage/relationship, family, social life, and leisure.

To create a vision book, first title each page with its corresponding sector of life. Under the title, you can tape or paste images or words that you have cut out from magazines that reflect what you want that area of your life to be like. You can use scrapbooking materials along with these images to create an uplifting visual representation that will support your goals and visions within that sector of your life. You are, in effect, turning each page into its own vision board.

During the workshops, I ask the women to work quickly and efficiently to create their vision books. I allow one full hour for this because we are creatures of habit and most of us would never start that task after we went home. If the women do not complete their vision books in that hour during the seminar, I encourage them to finish them at some point in the near future. I ask them to open their planners and schedule a time within the next week that is for themselves only. This time is not to be overridden by anything and should be treated as if it were a business meeting they cannot cancel.

In one of my workshops, ten minutes into the vision book exercise one of the ladies, who owned a fitness studio, stated that she needed to leave but promised to complete her vision book that night. I realized that I had forgotten to give her the SuperWoman certificate of completion that I hand out to those who attend the workshop. I emailed her to let her know I would be coming to her facility in a few days to work out and would bring along her certificate when I arrived at 5:30 p.m. To my surprise and delight, she wrote back to tell me that she would not be there because she had scheduled personal time with herself and was unable to break the appointment. She asked that I leave the certificate in her office. When I arrived, I proudly placed the certificate of completion on the SuperWoman's desk.

Later that evening, she sent me a picture of her completed vision book. I was beyond thrilled for her—and proud of myself too. Remember, SuperWomen are confident enough to give themselves credit and to share their stories of strength and the lessons they have learned so they can influence others in a positive way, which is what I had done. I may not have played a huge role in who this woman is today, but I did play a role in this specific experience in her life and it was empowering for us both.

Staying on Track

Now that you've finished reading this book and have set up some plans for working toward your own work-life balance, what's next? First, once you have participated in all the activities in this book and done so authentically, you can sign your SuperWoman certificate at the end of this chapter. (For a printable version, go to www.mindfulrehab.com and click on the link for "SuperWoman Worksheets.")

To help you continue creating your SuperWoman lifestyle, I've compiled a list of all the SuperWoman skills that you've been exploring in each chapter. In the process of self-searching and reformulating your goals, you may have identified additional traits that you feel are characteristics of a SuperWoman. Add the characteristics you come up with to the list below or in your journal.

How can you use this list? I encourage you to print out a copy and keep it somewhere visible so you are consistently reminded to work toward personal fulfillment and self-actualization. I suggest that you select two or three characteristics from this list, highlight them on your copy, and begin to work toward enhancing those aspects of yourself. When you feel that you have established a good momentum on incorporating new strategies and habits that will allow you to develop those two characteristics and you are ready to take on more, go back to the list and choose the next two skills you want to work on. Review the chapter and activities that correspond to those skills to remind yourself of the daily or weekly actions you need to take to reinforce your new habits.

SuperWoman, you are ready to take flight. You now have in hand the strategies you need to continue creating your SuperWoman lifestyle. I hope that in these pages you have discovered the self-awareness, self-confidence, and strength that will propel you toward a super-fulfilled life. Have fun with the new, fulfilled you!

~

The secret of change is to focus all of your energy not on fighting the old, but on building the new.

— DAN MILLMAN

SUPERWOMAN SKILLS

I focus on my top life roles.

A SuperWoman has identified her top five life roles and makes sure she is number one on that list.

A SuperWoman focuses on giving 100 percent to her top five roles.

A SuperWoman understands the differences between "kindness" and "doormat."

A SuperWoman does not feel guilty saying no to people who have mistaken her for a doormat.

A SuperWoman sets boundaries with all people, even spouses, children, and co-workers.

A SuperWoman makes time to enjoy the moments with those she loves and cares about most.

A SuperWoman understands that she can do anything she wants, but she can't do everything.

★ ★ ★

I call on my confidence as a core strength.

A SuperWoman makes her own decisions.

A SuperWoman speaks out loud and to herself
in ways that build her self-confidence.

A SuperWoman leads with
confidence instead of aggression.

A SuperWoman knows that she
doesn't have to be perfect.

A SuperWoman doesn't make impulsive decisions.

A SuperWoman highlights and stays aware
of her past and recent successes.

I identify and work through the real barriers to my fulfillment.

A SuperWoman accepts that there will be barriers on her journey toward success and fulfillment.

A SuperWoman is aware of and understands what barriers she frequently encounters.

A SuperWoman has a plan to work through her barriers.

A SuperWoman controls her actions and reactions.

A SuperWoman knows that she cannot control others. She can guide them, but she can't drive their car for them.

A SuperWoman compartmentalizes her frustrations.

A SuperWoman recognizes where her frustrations are coming from and works not to displace her anger onto those undeserving of that behavior.

I enjoy my life.

A SuperWoman is comfortable being comfortable.

A SuperWomen changes her mindset toward prevention.

A SuperWoman knows that her body and mind
are her most valuable tools in life and cares for them.

A SuperWoman rewards herself every day.

A SuperWoman works toward fulfilling
her own bucket list.

I create SMART goals to work toward fulfillment.

A SuperWoman makes sure the goals she sets are
specific, measureable, attainable, relevant, and *time-bound.*

A SuperWoman uses confidence to achieve goals.

A SuperWoman prioritizes and keeps in mind
her life roles when setting and working on her goals.

A SuperWoman knows that she does not need
to work on all her life goals at once.

A SuperWoman understands that personal or professional
support systems increase her chances of being successful.

A SuperWoman accepts constructive feedback
and does not internalize criticism from negative people.

A SuperWoman does not give up but finds
creative solutions to keep working toward her goals.

★ ★ ★

I track my progress toward my goals.

A SuperWoman writes down her goals and
consistently tracks her successes.

A SuperWoman does not compare herself to others
as she sets goals and tracks her progress.

A SuperWoman rewards herself when she
meets small and large goals.

A SuperWoman strives for
self-actualization, not perfection.

A SuperWoman does not live in crisis mode.

A SuperWoman retreats, rethinks, and then reacts as her
primary method for decision making.

A SuperWoman reframes her negativity to
remind herself that she does have choices and control.

I welcome and ask for support.

A SuperWoman takes time to assess
the people in her life.

A SuperWoman develops healthy support systems.

A SuperWoman stays away from negative people.

A SuperWoman rids herself of toxic people or
sets appropriate boundaries with them.

A SuperWoman accepts honest feedback about
her behavior and attitude from her valued supports.

★ ★ ★

**I reframe my life story to work for me
in positive ways in the present.**

A SuperWoman has identified and
embraces her true story.

A SuperWoman tells her story in a manner
that reflects strength and resilience.

A SuperWoman lets go of grudges, knowing that
they only hurt her and hold her back.

A SuperWoman knows that she isn't lucky
and that she has earned what she has.

A SuperWoman doesn't ask people to
bring balloons to her pity party.

A SuperWoman uses what she has learned from her own
challenging experiences to support and teach others.

OFFICIAL

SUPERWOMAN

This certificate hereby confers upon

_____

The license of
SUPERWOMAN

Specialization in Work-Life Balance

_____

DATE

ACKNOWLEDGMENTS

∾

I would like to thank my wonderful husband, Wes Kulaga, and sons, Wesley and Blake Kulaga, for their ongoing support while I was writing this book, allowing me the time I needed to pursue my life passion. They were so patient and understanding when I had to say no to certain activities so that I could write, and my husband was always willing to take over necessary family tasks so that I could pursue my dream.

A big thank you as well to Patricia Spadaro and to Nigel Yorwerth of Yorwerth Associates. They were instrumental in coaching me through the writing and editing process and shaping my book. They have continuously believed in me and encouraged me. Their expert guidance and support through all aspects of publishing, including their remarkable foreign rights representation, have been invaluable.

Dr. Jaime Kulaga is a licensed mental health counselor, certified professional coach, inspirational speaker, and entrepreneur. She is a frequent mental health expert on TV and has been featured on Forbes.com, on Maria Shriver's blog, and in *Glamour, Self,* and *Prevention* magazines for her expertise in work-life balance and life fulfillment. Dr. Kulaga's passion is to motivate others to live their best life. She coaches and counsels individuals, couples, and businesses and teaches at the university level. Her successful SuperWoman workshops empower women to make better decisions, steer the course of their lives, and use practical tools to find deeper fulfillment and happiness. To learn more about Dr. Jaime Kulaga and her work, visit www.mindfulrehab.com.